Soccer Made Easy

From Fundamental Skills to Championship Play

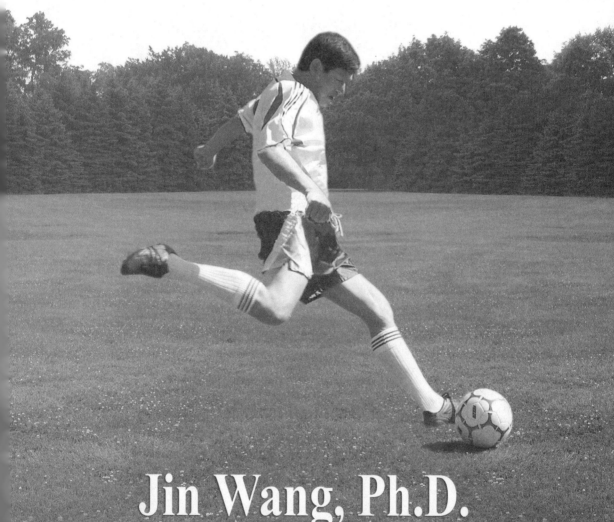

Jin Wang, Ph.D.
Kennesaw State University
Atlanta, USA

SOCCER MADE EASY: *FROM FUNDAMENTAL SKILLS TO CHAMPIONSHIP PLAY* / JIN WANG

Copyright © 2006, Ameriscietific, Inc. Kennesaw, GA 30152 USA

ISBN: 0-9778995-0-0

PRINTED IN THE UNITED STATES OF AMERICA

Library of Congress Cataloging-in-Publication Data

Soccer made easy: from fundamental skills to championship play / Jin Wang – 1st ed.

Contact Information of the Publishing Company:

Ameriscientific, Inc.
1418 Hampton Crest Dr. NW
Kennesaw, GA 30152 USA
Phone: (770) 419 - 6161 (Domestic and International)
Fax: (678) 392 - 3235
Website: www.optimalsoccer.com

Brief Contents

Table of Contents

Chapter 10. Ball Control Skills 179

Chapter 11. Basic Tactics and Strategies 193

Chapter 12. Basic Principles of Soccer Game 217

Preface

Without skills, there are no strategies in soccer.

Soccer is becoming increasingly popular among young people, from pre-kindergarten through college level. The rapid development of youth soccer programs has resulted in a huge gap between the fast-growing number of soccer players and the number of qualified soccer coaches. The shortage of qualified soccer coaches has become an obstacle to the healthy development of soccer programs.

Teaching soccer skills is not value free. If taught improperly, soccer players can develp bad habits that affect further development of skill acquisition, eventually leading to poor performance and, in turn, affecting their interest in playing the sport. In fact, players' interest in soccer largely depends on their own perception of how competent they are in soccer (Harter, 1978, 1981). Coaches, parents, and practitioners have an unavoidable responsibility to provide quality coaching for youngsters to ensure they learn soccer skills and enjoy games. The increasing popularity of soccer has led to the publication of various soccer books to help kids and students learn how to play soccer; each of these books has its own strengths and weaknesses, with some focusing on basic concepts of soccer skills and strategies, and others being filled with a large volume of text focusing upon highly specific skills. Unfortunately, most available soccer books highlight only limited soccer techniques as examples of how to learn soccer skills. As a result, students are unable to obtain a comprehensive learning guide for a full spectrum of soccer techniques. According to soccer regulations, a soccer player can use every part of his/her body except arms and hands to contact the ball. Therefore, a competent soccer player should learn many different skills to play effectively. Thus, a book that presents a full sequence of soccer skills and techniques will be truly helpful in assisting soccer lovers accomplish their goals of learning comprehensive skills and techniques.

The strengths of this book are that it (1) provides an easy-to-learn approach with use of extensive visual illustrations to highlight important soccer techniques without requiring the reading of extensive text to understand the concepts; (2) is a comprehensive soccer skill-learning book, clearly explaining a full range of Olympic soccer skill learning processes; (3) can be used by novices and advanced players, soccer coaches, parents and practitioners; (4) explains the key elements of soccer skills; (5) elaborates on the core principles of soccer games and strategies of play; and (6) illustrates the roles of each position and interpretations of major soccer rules. Beyond that, each chapter emphasizes the most important learning principles such as the name and purpose of the technique, key elements to remember, common mistakes of the skill, pictures of the skill, and design of practice. A thorough understanding of soccer skill learning concepts will allow coaches, parents and practitioners to provide soccer players with more effective instruction and help them master Olympic soccer skills.

This book is divided into thirteen chapters; the first ten chapters discuss the soccer techniques and learning strategies. Each of the particular soccer skill categories is further divided into many sub-skills that allow coaches, athletes, parents, and practitioners to gain an overall understanding of a comprehensive progression of a learning sequence for a particular skill. In this way, soccer athletes can learn skills through a systematic and gradual approach. The last three chapters deal with the areas of tactical aspects, formation analysis, characteristics of field zone, styles of play, role of each position, strategies of play and the like. Because of comprehensive nature of this book, soccer athletes from novice to advanced players, and educators from parents to coaches can all use "Soccer Made Easy." This book is also suitable for colleges and high schools, YMCAs, soccer clubs, and many soccer organizations to use in the development of soccer skills. I am excited that this book will be able to assist so many soccer lovers to develop their comprehensive soccer skills. During your learning process, if you have any suggestions or comments for improving this book, please e-mail me at the following address: wang566@gmail.com. Good luck in your endeavors to become a successful soccer player and an effective soccer coach!

Foreword

I am honored to write this foreword for Dr. Jin Wang's book. Featuring high-quality photo illustrations along with concise language, this is an exceptional introductory reading on soccer. With its succinct, easy-to-understand explanations of the technical skills of soccer, this book will prove instrumental in helping soccer lovers, especially younger players, to master the fundamental skills and maneuvers of soccer.

With his great achievements in the sport of soccer, Dr. Wang is not only an exceptional athlete and coach, but also a renowned researcher in Sports Sciences. He has been a featured speaker at international soccer conferences and a regular contributor to international sports journals, which is a strong testament to his knowledge and insights in soccer. Well grounded in theory but focusing on the practical aspects of soccer, Dr. Wang's book explains the complicated principles of soccer maneuvers in simple terms, leading his readers down an enlightening path to the essence of this sport.

Among the many books currently available on soccer, this book is one of a kind. I am thrilled to know it will be circulated internationally. I sincerely wish Dr. Wang great success with this book and in further advancing the sport of soccer.

Yuan-An Ma

Former Head Coach of the Chinese Olympic Women's Soccer Team, that won the second place for the 1999 Women's Soccer World Cup

Dedicated to:

This book is dedicated to:

▶ My father, **Yue Ting Wang,** who believes in me and teaches me to achieve the goals I set.

▶ My mother, **Xie Jiao Yue** (1922 – 1997), who was a great mom.

▶ My wife, **Xiao Lan Xu**, who continuously gives me support.

▶ My children, **Anna Wang, Jennifer Wang, and Bryan Wang**, who enlighten my life and give me all the joy I can dream of.

Acknowledgements

It has been a challenging process to complete this book. Many people have made contributions to this project, and I would like to take this opportunity to extend my personal and sincere thanks to the following individuals:

Mrs. Xiao Lan Xu – I can't thank my wife enough for her long-term support and encouragement of this project. As an amateur photographer, you took most of these photos during many hot and cold days. This book reflects much of your effort and support.

Dr. John David Johnson – Many thanks for your goalie demonstrations that are well reflected in the book. Also, your photo-taking skills are impressive. I truly appreciate your assistance and support on this project.

Mr. James Bolt – As a professional photographer, you have used your considerable talent to convert textual theory into visual art. The certain sections of the photos you took have become an important part of this book.

Dr. Ruth A. Goldfine – Many thanks for your final editing and proofreading.

Dr. Mitchell Collins – Thank you for your assistance and support on this project. You are always resourceful and have been a great colleague to work with.

Dr. John McLester – Your positive attitude and enlightening spirit are contagious. It is fun to work with you. Thanks for your assistance and support on this project.

Mr. Yi Lin Shen – Many thanks for your long-time encouragement and support.

Ms. Breanna Jacinto Johnson –Thank you for taking some photos for the project during the cold weather.

Chapter 1: Getting Started

Basic Knowledge of the Soccer Ball

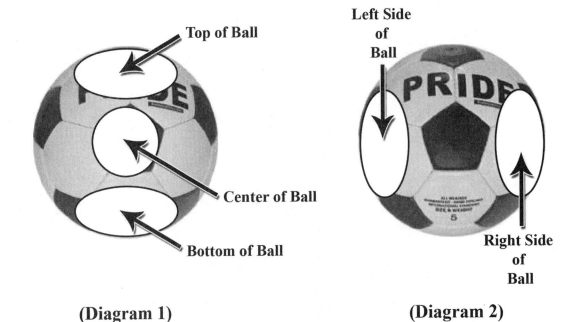

(Diagram 1)

(Diagram 2)

Explanation

The purpose of playing soccer is to manipulate the ball by using certain parts of the foot to contact a particular part of the ball at any given time. According to the principles of force, there are three elements of force that a soccer player has to manipulate: (1) magnitude, (2) direction, and (3) point of contact of the force upon the object. For example, in a kicking situation, a soccer player must control how much force should be used, which direction to kick to, and where to contact the ball. Thus, a competent soccer player must first study the characteristics of the ball. From a back view, the ball can be divided into five sections: the top and bottom of the ball, left side and right side of the ball, and center of the ball. Once a player has decided how much force to apply and which direction to kick to, the player must contact the correct part of the ball in order to kick the ball to the intended position. Incorrect contact could propel the ball out of control. Thus, in order to understand the characteristics of the ball and have great control of the three elements of force, soccer players should engage in extensive ball control skill training. Familiarity with the personality of the ball, such as where to make contact, how much force to use and in which direction to apply that force, will lead to much more effective play.

Obviously, when playing soccer, a player may kick the ball from left side, right side, or front. Therefore, the concept of the five sections of a soccer ball presented above in the back-view example can be applied to the other three sides (i.e., left, right and back). The above illustration visually depicts the available contact points options of the soccer ball.

Basic Knowledge of the Foot

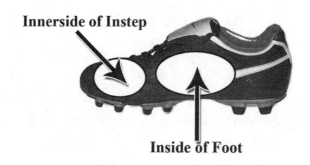

(Diagram 3)

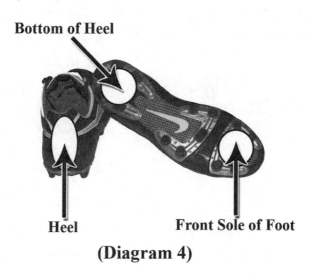

(Diagram 4)

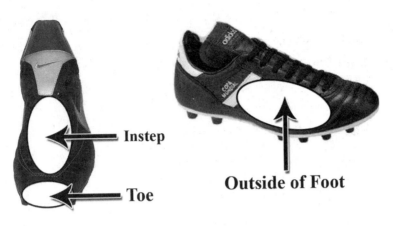

Instep

Toe

Outside of Foot

(Diagram 5)

▶ **Explanation**

A soccer player generally contacts the ball with the foot by using one of the seven areas at any given time in competition. These places are the inside of foot, outside of foot, innerside of foot, instep, toe, back of foot, and front sole of foot. Each of these places has a unique use for the specific play. For example, the inside of foot is used for a short distance pass because accuracy is increased with a large contact area. The weakness of this type of kick includes the limited range of kicking motion and slow speed of kicking due to an inconvenient anatomical leg position. Therefore, this type of kick is unable to generate large forces. Thus, the inside of foot kick is best used for passing. Conversely, the instep kick not only has a large contact area to the ball, but also the player can swing his/her kicking leg with an extremely large range of motion. Therefore, the instep kick is best used for shooting. Soccer players should carefully study each of the above contact areas of the foot so that he/she can properly maneuver the ball at a particular time and a particular situation.

Basic Knowledge of Body Contact Areas to the Ball

According to the soccer regulations, a soccer player can contact ball with every body part except the arms and hands. Obviously, a goalie can use all body parts including arms and hands within the penalty area in competition. However, the question is: "can a soccer player effectively use all these body parts to gain advantages in competition?" The answer is "no." Many of body parts can not be effectively used to contact the ball for game advantages such as a player's back of the body, back of the leg, hip, etc. Thus, using certain designated body parts to contact the ball in competition is a necessary learning strategy to effectively play soccer. A soccer learner must fully understand which body parts can be used effectively to maneuver the ball during competition; therefore, they must spend a great deal of time practicing these skills during training. Generally speaking, soccer players constantly use the following body parts to contact the ball based on the particular game situation and circumstance: head, shoulder, chest, thigh, inside of foot, outside of foot, instep, innerside of foot, toe, heel and sole of foot. Among these body parts, some of them are used more often than others. For example, shoulders, toe and heel are rarely used by novice soccer players in competition, but they might be used quite often by more advanced players. The following photos illustrate each of the body contact areas for kicking, trapping, dribbling, heading, beating opponent, etc. Every player must constantly practice soccer drills by using each of these body parts in order to perfect soccer skills. Being able to swiftly maneuver the soccer ball with ease by using different parts of the body and feet, a soccer player can achieve peak performance in competition. Therefore, soccer players should have a full understanding of appropriate ball contact based on the game situation. The following illustrations help soccer players to know the correct body parts with which to make contact.

(a) Inside of the Foot

(b) Innerside of the Foot

(c) Instep

(d) Outside of the Foot

(e) Toe

(f) Back of the Foot

(g) Sole of the Foot

(h) Thigh

(i) Chest

(j) Forehead

(k) Shoulder

Symbols

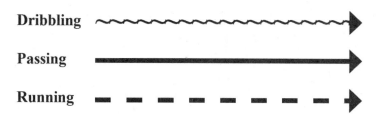

Dribbling

Passing

Running

(Diagram 6)

Chapter 2: Kicking

Introduction

Soccer is a sport in which all different parts of the body can be used, except the hands for the field players. Because soccer players use their feet most of the time, the sport is called football in most of the world. Since soccer is a dynamic sport, players can use different types of kicks based on game situation. For example, a player can make a short pass, long pass, curved pass, shoot, or chip the ball into the air, and so on. A player will choose the most suitable kicks to accomplish his/her goal based on the particular game situation and his/her position.

There are six different ways of kicking: (1) inside of foot pass, (2) innerside of instep kick, (3) instep kick, (4) outside of foot kick, (5) toe kick, and (6) heel kick. Each of these kicks has unique characteristics and is used for specific purposes. Consequently soccer players must learn the different types of kicks so they can play the game effectively. Three kicking skills are used most often by soccer players in competition: inside of foot pass, innerside of instep kick, and instep kick. However, at the elite level, the outside of foot kick has been used quite often, but it is a skill that requires extensive training for a player to use it effectively. Toe and heel kicks are not used as often as the rest of the kicking skills.

Shooting practice should be emphasized significantly, but effective shooting can prove to be difficult to execute during competition. Coaches must arrange various practices from easy approaches to the most competitive ones (Wang, 2004). Once reaching the advanced level of training, the shooting practice arrangements must involve in defenders around the shooter so that the conditions of practice are similar to the game situations (Wang, 1999).

The following are the six different ways of kicking and each of the sections includes the purpose and the technique of the kicking, the common mistakes, the pictures of the demonstration and the practice arrangement. With a comprehensive understanding of each of these kicking techniques, soccer players can master the fundamental kicking techniques in order to play game more effectively.

Six Ways of Kicking

(1) Inside of Foot kicking

▶ **Purpose of Inside of Foot Kicking**

The inside of foot passing is mainly used for short distance passes because its large area of contact on the ball provides great accuracy. Generally speaking, soccer players use the inside of foot pass more than seventy percent of the time in a game. Players from novice to elite level must effectively master this particular skill.

▶ **Technique for Inside of Foot Kicking**

- Approach the ball straight on, running at a moderate speed.

- Place the support foot beside the ball with the toe pointing forward.

- Swing the lower leg of the kicking limb.

- <u>Contact the ball with the inside of the kicking foot perpendicular to the support foot</u>.

- <u>Keep the kicking foot parallel to the ground</u>.

- Follow through with minimum motion.

- Contact the center of the ball with the foot.

▶ **Key Elements to Remember**

- <u>Keep the kicking foot perpendicular to the supporting foot</u>.

- <u>Keep the kicking foot parallel to the ground.</u>

► **Common Mistakes**

- Kicking foot is not perpendicular to the support foot.

- The sole of the kicking foot is not parallel to the ground.

- The support foot stands behind the ball instead of beside the ball.

► **Pictures of Inside of Foot Passing**

(a) Approach the ball

(b) Swing lower leg

(c) Contact the ball with inside of foot

(d) Pass a smooth ground ball

(e) Side view – inside of foot passing   **(f) Front view – inside of foot passing**

▶ **Practicing Inside of Foot Passing**

1) Keep feet perpendicular to one another and keep the kicking foot parallel to the ground.

2) Swing the kicking foot without a ball.

3) Practice the entire kicking motion without a ball.

4) Pass ground ball between two players with a distance of ten to fifteen yards (Diagram 7).

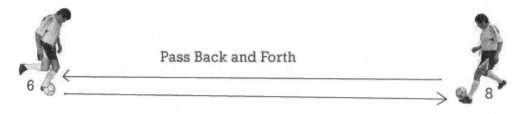

Pass Back and Forth

6   8

(Diagram 7)

5) Players 5 and 6 pass a ball back and forth within an 80-degree arc-shaped area. Player 5 is stationary and passes the ball to Player 6 who runs back and forth in an 80-degree arc (Diagram 8).

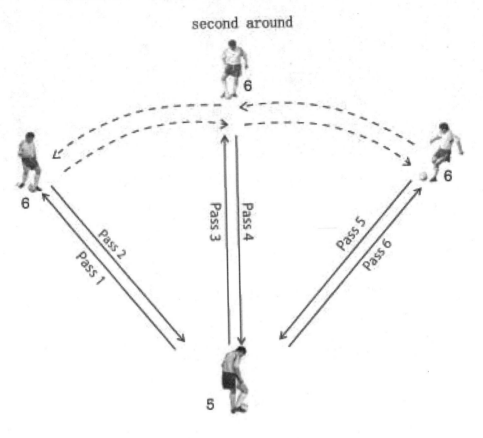

(Diagram 8)

6) Players 2, 3, and 4 stand in a triangle position to pass the ball from each other (Diagram 9).

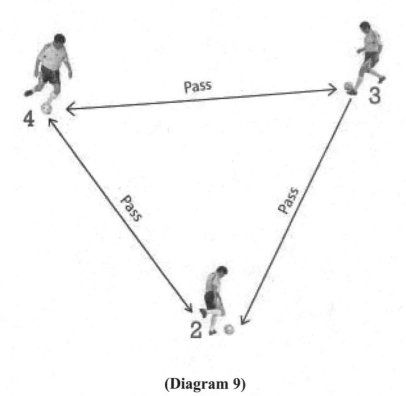

(Diagram 9)

7) Player 2 passes a ball to players 3, 4, 5, and 6 back and forth within an 80-degree arc-shaped area (Diagram 10).

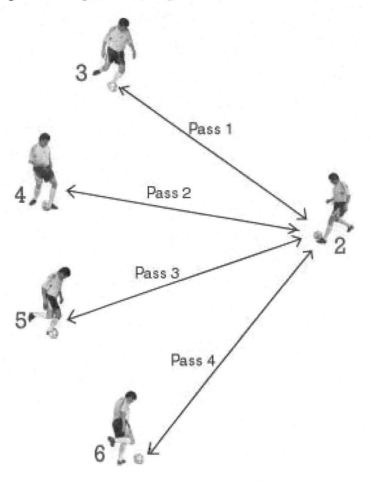

(Diagram 10)

8) Players 5 and 7 pass a ball back and forth and players 6 and 8 do the same. Both groups must pass the balls with a good timing to avoid the balls colliding with each other (Diagram 11).

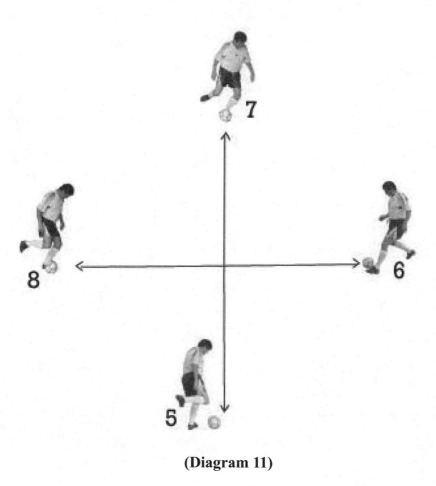

(Diagram 11)

9) Player 6 passes a ball to player 5 who passes the ball back to player 6 who turns around his/her body to dribble the ball forward, then makes a 180° turn to dribble the ball backward for 10 yards and cut the ball backward and dribble the ball back and pass it to player 5 again Diagram 12).

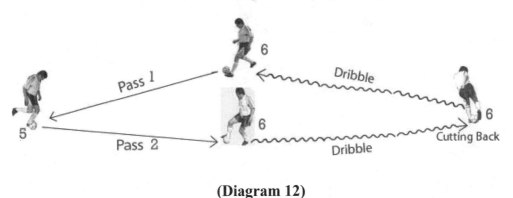

(Diagram 12)

10) Player 6 dribbles and passes the ball to player 8, who passes the ball back to player 6 again. The player 6 dribbles the ball forward (Diagram 13).

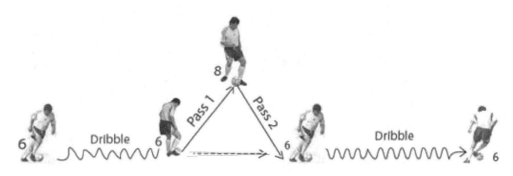

(Diagram 13)

11) Players 2, 3, and 7 stand in a line facing players 4, 5 and 6 who stand approximately ten yards away. Player 2 passes a ball to player 4 and immediately runs forward to stand behind player 6. As soon as player 4 sees the ball come, he/she passes it to player 3 and runs forward to stand behind player 7. Both groups pass the ball back and forth, keeping the ball on the ground (Diagram 14).

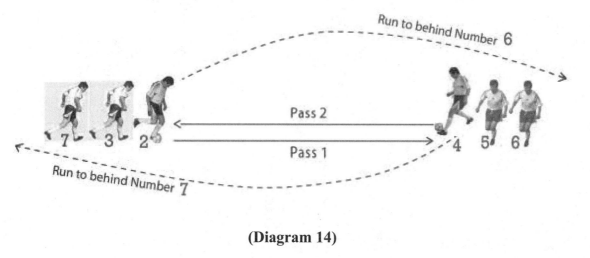

(Diagram 14)

12) Players 7 and 8 keep seven yards apart, facing the same direction and pass a ball to each other while slowly running forward (Diagram 15).

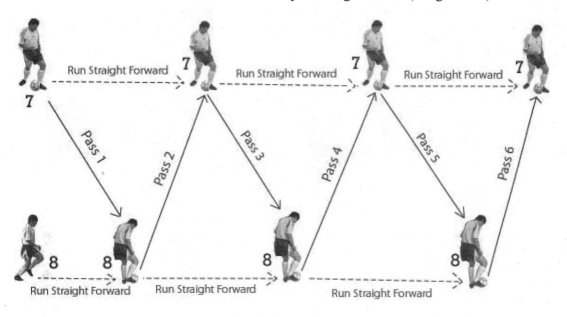

(Diagram 15)

13) Two players do the same as the above, but they pass the ball between the cones (Diagram 16).

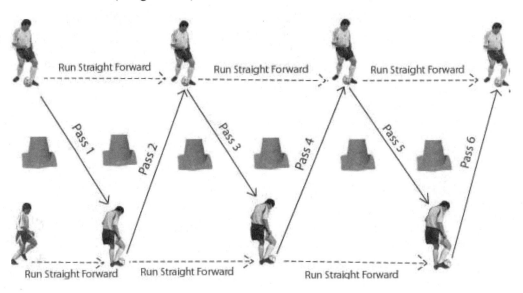

(Diagram 16)

14) Players 6 and 7 keep seven yards apart, facing the same direction, and player 7 dribbles the ball forward first, then passes it to player 6 who receives and dribbles the ball forward, then passes it to player 7 again. Both players repeat the same process (Diagram 17).

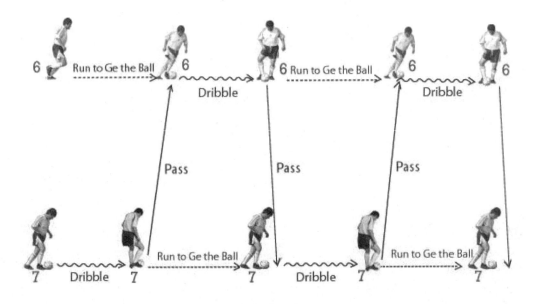

(Diagram 17)

15) Players 3, 4, and 5 stand in a row, seven feet apart from each other and facing the same direction. All three players slowly run forward while passing to each other. Player 3 laterally passes the ball to Player 4, who receives the ball and laterally passes the ball to Player 5 while all of them continue running forward (Diagram 18).

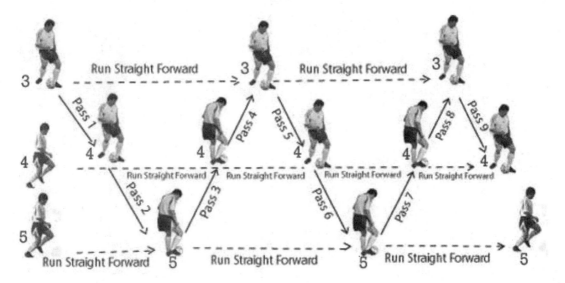

(Diagram 18)

16) Player 6 passes the ball straight to player 7, who runs from the opposite side of the position. Meanwhile, As soon as player 6 passed the ball to player 7, player 6 runs to the opposite side to receive the ball from player 7. Two players repeat the same process in order to practice the inside of foot pass (Diagram 19).

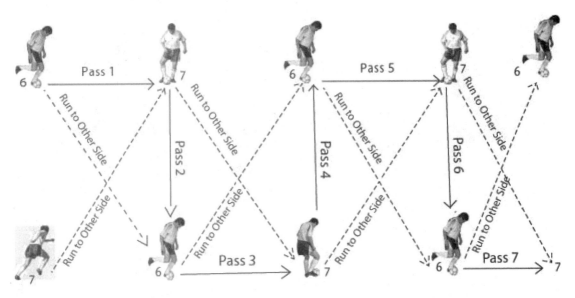

(Diagram 19)

17) Players 5 and 6 pass a ball back and forth between the various triangle obstacles within half of the field. The players should not hit the triangle obstacles during the process of passing (Diagram 20).

(Diagram 20)

(2) Instep Kicking

▶ **Purpose of Instep Kicking**

Instep kicking is mainly used for shooting because of its power and accuracy.

▶ **Technique for Instep Kicking**

- Approach the ball straight on, at a run, gradually increasing pace.

- Place support foot beside the ball while gradually extending the knee.

- Swing the kicking leg as fast as possible.

- Contact the ball with the instep while keeping the ankle extended and locked as firmly as possible.

- Provide maximum follow through.

▶ **Key Elements to Remember**

- <u>The last stride of the approach should be as large as possible.</u>

- <u>Swing the kicking foot as fast as possible.</u>

- <u>Extend and lock the kicking ankle as firmly as possible.</u>

- At the moment of contact, fully extend the knee of the support leg.

▶ **Common Mistakes**

- Have a small final stride of approach.

- The kicking ankle is not locked during the moment of the ball contact.

- Swing kicking leg slowly.

▶ **Pictures of Instep Kicking**

(a) Approach the ball   (b) Make a large final stride

(c) Swing kicking leg as fast as possible

(d) Place support foot beside the ball

(e) Contacts the ball with the instep

(f) Follow through

(f) Front view – instep shot

(h) Back view – instep shot

▶ Practicing Instep Kicking

1) Shoot the ball from a stationary position (Diagram 21 & 22).

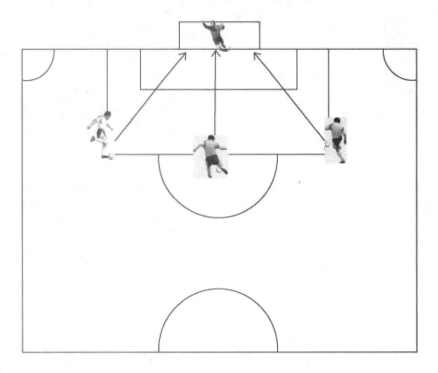

(Diagram 21)

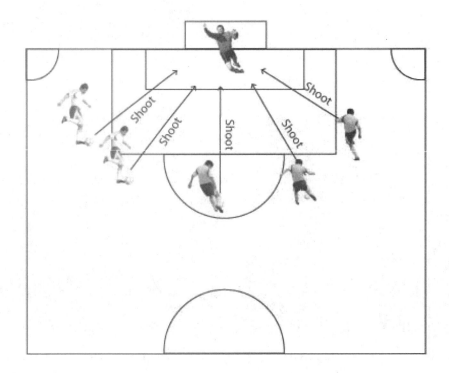

(Diagram 22)

2) Shoot the ball from three different positions with certain approach distance (Diagram 23).

(Diagram 23)

3) Dribble the ball forward to shoot (Diagram 24).

(Diagram 24)

4) Dribble a long distance before shooting (Diagram 25).

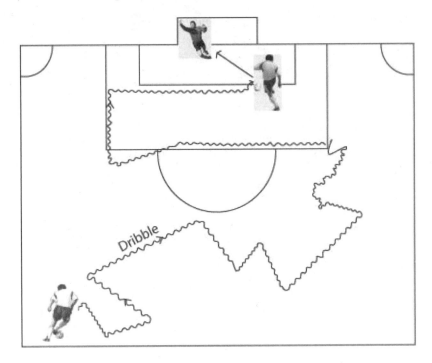

(Diagram 25)

5) Players 10 and 11 shoot the ball while running passed by a teammate (Diagram 26).

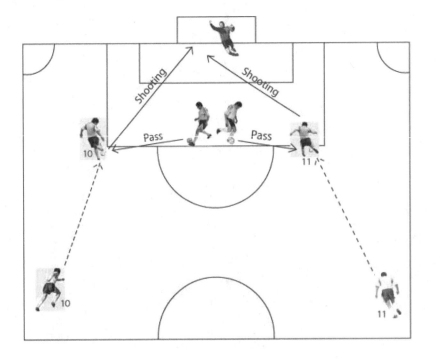

(Diagram 26)

6) Dribble the ball to an opposite position to shoot the ball with a sharp angle (Diagram 27).

(Diagram 27)

7) The offender dribbles the ball in a Z shaped path to shoot in the presence of a defender who always maintains a containing position (Diagram 28).

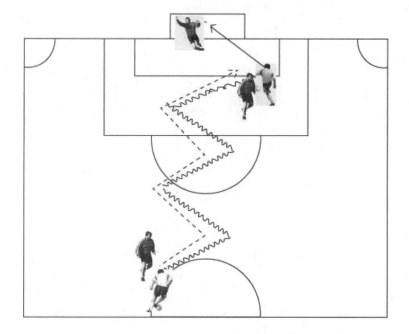

(Diagram 28)

8) Dribble to beat a defender and shoot (Diagram 29).

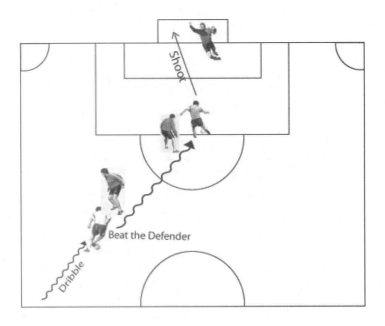

(Diagram 29)

9) Two players fight to get a fast rolling ball and the winner becomes an offender to shoot while the loser becomes a defender (Diagram 30).

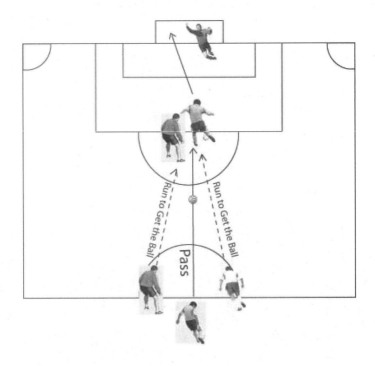

(Diagram 30)

10) Shooter dribbles the ball in the presence of a defender who keeps in a containing position all the time from three different directions (Diagram 31).

(Diagram 31)

11) The offender dribbles the ball forward with the two defenders present; one of whom is around the shooter and the other is in the front of the shooter. The shooter must handle the ball properly to shoot the ball. Repeat this practice from two different directions (Diagram 32).

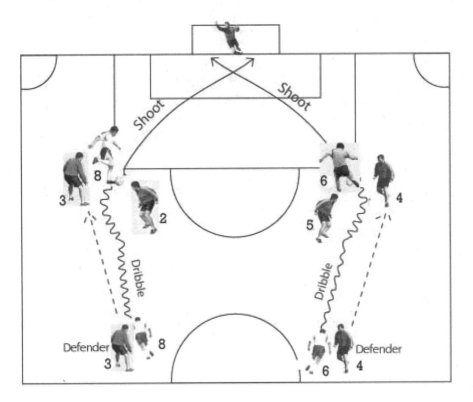

(Diagram 32)

12) The offender dribbles the ball down to the opposite position to shoot with a defender around him/her all the time. Repeat this practice from two different directions (Diagram 33).

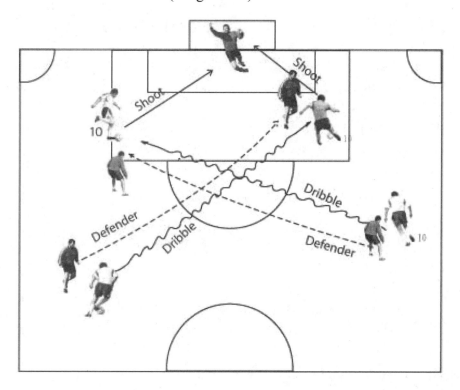

(Diagram 33)

(3) Innerside of Instep Kicking

▶ **Purpose of Innerside of Instep Kicking**

The innerside of instep kicking is mainly used for long distance passing or shooting.

▶ **Technique of Innerside of Instep Kicking**

- Approach the ball at a 45° angle in relation to a horizontal line.

- Place support foot beside and behind the ball.

- Kick the ball with the appropriate force for the intended distance of the kick.

- Contact the ball with the innerside of the instep with an outward position of the kicking foot, keeping the ankle locked.

- A proper follow through.

▶ **Key Elements to Remember**

- The last approach stride should be relatively large.

- Swing the kicking leg with the appropriate force necessary to achieve the purpose of the kick.

- Lock the ankle of the kicking foot as firmly as possible.

▶ **Common Mistakes**

- Have a small final stride of approach.

- The ankle of kicking foot is not locked.

- Swing the kicking leg slowly.

▶ **Pictures of Innerside of Instep Kicking**

(A) Innerside of instep kick for short distance pass

      (a) Approach the ball   **(b) Ready position before kicking**

(c) Contact the ball with
   innerside of instep

(d) Follow-through

(B) Pictures of Innerside of Instep Kick for Long Distance Pass

(a) Approach the ball (side view)

(b) Final stride of the approach phase
   (side view)

(c) The ball contact (front view)

(d) Follow through (Back View)

(g) Front view of the ball contact

(h) Back view of the ball contact - through

> ▶ **Practice for Innerside of Instep Kick**

> • Please see the section of the practicing instep kick.

(4) Outside of Foot Kicking

> ▶ **Purpose of Outside of Foot Kicking**

> The outside of foot kick is mainly used for shooting, passing, corner kicking, or long distance passing because of its deceptive nature and power.

> ▶ **Technique for Outside of Foot Kick**

- Approach the ball with a preferred position based on the player's desire.

- Place the support foot beside or a little behind the ball.

- Kick the ball with the appropriate force necessary for the intended distance of the kick.

- <u>Contact the ball with the outside of the foot keeping the ankle locked.</u>

- A proper follow through.

▶ **Common Mistakes**

- Have a small final stride of approach phase.

- Unable to keep in an inwarded position of the kicking foot.

- The ankle of the kicking foot is not locked.

▶ **Key Elements to Remember**

- <u>The last approach stride should be large.</u>

- Swing the kicking foot quickly.

- Lock the ankle of the kicking foot as firmly as possible.

- Extend the knee of the supporting leg at the time of contact.

► **Pictures of Outside of Foot Kicking**

(a) Approach the ball

(b) Large final stride of approach

(c) Contact to the ball

(d) Follow-through

► **Practice Outside of Foot Shooting**

Please see the pages xx - xx

(5)   Toe Kicking

► **Purpose of Toe Kicking**

Toe kicking is mainly used for short distance passing or shooting because of its quickness and deceptive nature.

► **Technique of Toe Kicking**

Kick the center of the ball using a quick motion.

▶ **Key Elements to Remember**

Use a small, quick motion to kick the ball to make a short pass or to shoot.

▶ **Picture of Toe Kick**

(6) Heel Kicking

▶ **Purpose of Heel Kicking**

The heel kick is mainly used to pass the ball backward because of its deceptive nature.

▶ **Technique for Heel Kicking**

Kick the ball with heel with a quick motion.

▶ **Picture of Heel Kicking**

Chapter 3: Trapping and Receiving

Introduction

Trapping skills are more challenging to learn than kicking skills because of their passive nature and unpredictable incoming ball. In other words, an athlete has no control of when and where the ball will come. A player's decision as to how to trap the ball must be based on the direction, speed, and position of the incoming ball so that he/she can decide how and when to trap the ball. During competition, an incoming ball may come from different directions at various speeds and formats. For example, a ball could be high or low, have spin or no spin, a curve or not curve, and travel from various directions taking different trajectories. No matter where, when, and how the ball is coming, a soccer player must trap and control the ball immediately within a controllable perimeter. To accomplish that, the athlete must effectively use the proper body part to trap the ball.

A player can use his/her chest, head, thigh, and different parts of the foot to trap the ball. The technique used depends on the situation of the incoming ball. For example, to trap a high incoming ball, the athlete should use the chest trap; similarly, an incoming ball at thigh level should be trapped with the player's thigh. Another factor affecting which trapping technique should be used is the immediate surrounding situation such as the opponents' position(s), potential open area for the next movement after trapping, receivers' position, and so forth. The trapper must bring the ball to under his/her control in a manner that sets up his/her next move.

Soccer players often use the inside of foot trap, thigh trap, or chest trap because these body parts after a large contact area with the ball for maximum control. An athlete must spend a great deal of time practicing trapping in order to perfect this skill for effective use in competition. Trapping the ball in competition is the first move prior to engaging in passing, shooting, dribbling, or other activities. Without competent trapping skills, an athlete will have to chase the ball around all the time in competition. Unfortunately, many athletes are not aware of the importance of trapping skills because trapping is perceived as a non-offensive play and is easily overlooked by coaches and athletes. This resulted in players who cannot play and enjoy the game effectively. Practicing trapping is an essential skill that should be given great priority and attention.

Types of Trapping

(1) Trapping a Ground Ball

▶ **Purpose of Trapping a Ground Ball**

The main purpose of trapping a ground ball is to receive an incoming ground ball and establish possession.

▶ **Technique for Trapping a Ground Ball**

- Keep feet perpendicular to one another.

- Use the inside of the foot to trap the ball, moving the foot backward at a speed consistent with that of the incoming ball until the ball stops.

▶ **Key Elements to Remember**

- The backswing motion of the trapping foot should be consistent with the speed of the incoming ball.

▶ **Pictures of Trapping a Ground Ball**

(a) Move the trapping foot forward to prepare for contact with the ball

(b) Before contacting the ball

(c) Inside of the foot contacts the ball and moves backward with the ball

(d) Trap the ball to the intended position

▶ **Practicing Trapping a Ground Ball**

1) Practice the backswing motion of the foot without a ball.

2) Trap a slow incoming ball.

3) Trap a fast incoming ball.

4) After trapping, execute the next movement (diagram 34).

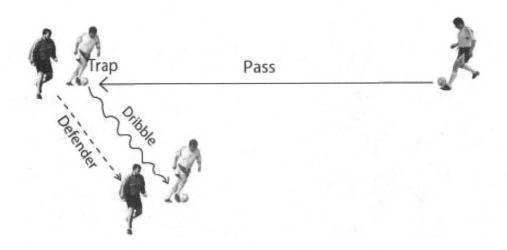

(Diagram 34)

5) Trap a ground ball with an opponent around.

(2) Chest Trapping

▶ **Purpose of Chest Trapping**

Chest trapping is used to trap an incoming ball that is chest high. There are two different ways to trap the ball; one is to trap a relative high ball, and another is to trap a flat and forceful ball that is chest high.

(2.a) Chest Trapping a High Ball

▶ **Technique for Chest Trapping a High Ball**

Prepare to trap the ball with the chest by first putting the trunk of the body in an arch-shaped position. Inhale a breath and hold it preparation for trapping. Trap the ball while on tip-toe and pop bounce the ball up and then control the ball on the ground with the foot.

▶ **Key Elements to Remember**

- Keep the upper-body in an arch-shaped position while trapping.

- Keep your chin down.

- Pop bounce the ball upward.

▶ **Common Mistakes**

- Closing eyes and keeping arms down.

▶ **Pictures of Chest Trapping a High Ball**

<table>
<tr><td>(a) Watch the incoming ball</td><td>(b) Prepare for trapping</td></tr>
</table>

(c) Trap the ball with the chest

(d) Trap the ball and prepare for next movement

(e) Prepare to control the ball with the foot

(f) Control the ball with the inside of the foot

(2.b) Chest Trap a Powerful Ball

▶ **Technique for Chest Trapping a Powerful Ball**

Move the chest backwards to absorb the force of the incoming ball, contacting the ball with either the left or right side of the chest to bring the ball down.

▶ **Key Elements to Remember**

• Trap the ball with ideal timing.

• Trap the ball with one side of chest (male athlete) or the upper center of the chest (female athlete).

▶ **Common Mistakes**

- Closed eyes.

- Improper timing.

▶ **Pictures of Chest Trapping a Power Ball**

(a) Watch the incoming ball

(b) Trap the ball with the chest

(c) Immediately move chest backward

(d) Prepare for next movement

(e) Trap the ball with the inside of the foot

▶ **Practicing Chest Trapping**

1) Practice the trapping motion without the ball.

2) Toss the ball into the air, and then trap the ball with the chest (Diagram 35).

(Diagram 35)

3) Chest trap the ball tossed by a partner (Diagram 36).

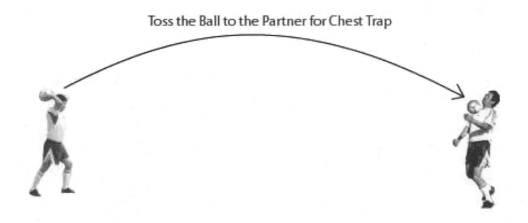

Toss the Ball to the Partner for Chest Trap

(Diagram 36)

4) Chest trap the ball kicked by a partner (Diagram 37 and 38).

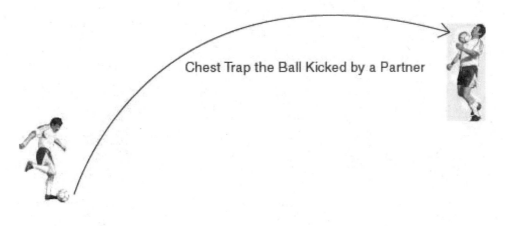

Chest Trap the Ball Kicked by a Partner

(Diagram 37)

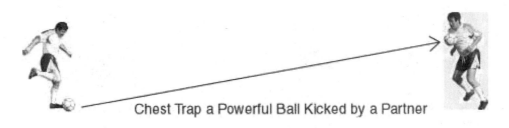

Chest Trap a Powerful Ball Kicked by a Partner

(Diagram 38)

5) Trap the incoming ball kicked by a partner while running (Diagram 39).

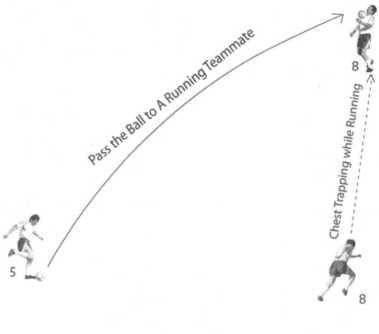

(Diagram 39)

6) Trap the incoming ball with an opponent around (Diagram 40).

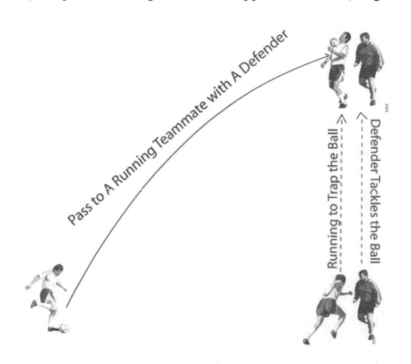

(Diagram 40)

(3) Thigh Trapping

▶ **Purpose of Thigh Trapping**

Thigh trapping is used to maneuver an incoming ball at thigh level to a controllable position.

▶ **Technique for Thigh Trapping**

- Raise the thigh and trap the incoming ball with the center of the thigh.

- As soon as the ball reaches the thigh, the thigh should be moved backward at a speed consistent with the speed of the incoming ball.

▶ **Key Elements to Remember**

- Use the center of the thigh to trap the ball.

- Move the thigh with ideal timing.

▶ **Common Mistakes**

Moving the trapping leg too slowly or too quickly.

▶ **Pictures of Thigh Trapping**

(a) Approach the ball to find the right position

(b) Raise the thigh to receive the ball

(c) Move the thigh backward

(d) Trap the ball to the intended position

▶ **Practicing Thigh Trapping**

1) Two hands hold the ball and place the ball on thigh to sense the ball contact position.

2) Practice thigh trapping without the ball.

3) Toss a ball into the air and trap the ball with the thigh (Diagram 41).

(Diagram 41)

4) Thigh trap the ball tossed by a partner (Diagram 42).

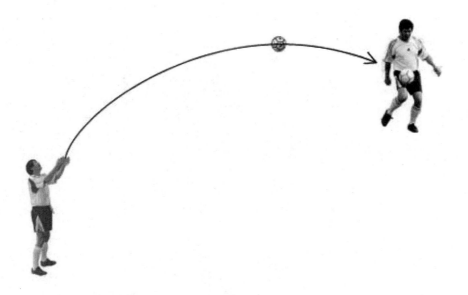

(Diagram 42)

5) Thigh trap the ball kicked by a partner (Diagram 43).

Pass the Ball to A Partner for Thigh Trap

(Diagram 43)

6) Thigh trap the ball with an opponent around (Diagram 44).

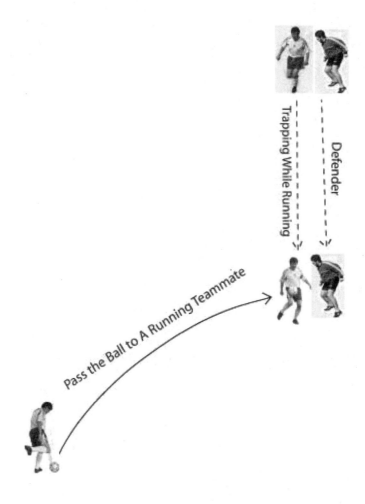

Trapping While Running

Defender

Pass the Ball to A Running Teammate

(Diagram 44)

(4) Trapping an Air-Ball Beside the Body

▶ **Purpose of Trapping an Air-Ball Beside the Body**

The purpose of trapping an air-ball beside the body is to receive the air-ball on either side of the body to a controllable position.

▶ **Technique of Trapping an Air-Ball Beside the Body**

Trapping an air-ball coming on either side of the body using the inside of the foot to contact the ball and bring it down to a controllable position.

▶ **Key Elements to Remember**

- Anticipate when and where the ball will reach the trapper.

- Place the trapping foot in the proper position with perfect timing to bring the ball to a controllable position.

▶ **Pictures of Trapping an Air-Ball Beside the Body**

(a) Find the right position

(b) ready position

(c) Receive the ball with the inside of the foot

(d) Bring the ball down

▶ **Practicing Trapping an Air-ball Beside the Body**

1) Practice trapping an air-ball beside the body without using a ball.

2) Trap an incoming ball with an opponent around.

3) Trap the air-ball tossed by a partner (Diagram 45).

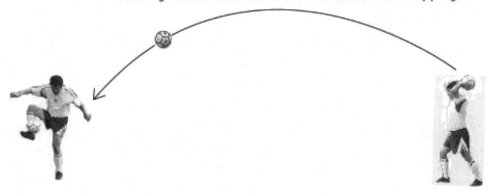

Throwing the Ball to a Partner for the Inside of Foot Trapping

(Diagram 45)

4) Trap the air-ball kicked by a partner (Diagram 46).

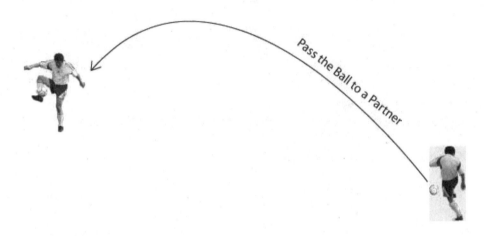

Pass the Ball to a Partner

(Diagram 46)

5) Trap the incoming air-ball with an opponent around (Diagram 47).

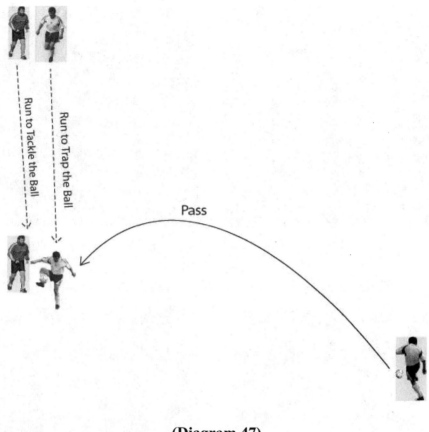

(Diagram 47)

(5) Trapping a Bouncing Ball

▶ **Purpose of Trapping a Bouncing Ball**

The purpose of Trapping a Bouncing Ball is to control a high ball that has hit the ground.

▶ **Technique of Trapping a Bouncing Ball**

As soon as the ball hits the ground, trap the ball with the sole of the foot, place the inside or outside of the foot on the upper-side of the ball with a gentle motion.

▶ **Key Elements to Remember**

- Trap the ball instead of kicking it.

- Contact the ball with precise timing, not to delay or miss the ball.

(a) Find the right position to trap the ball

(b) The ready position

(c) Keep the toe up and use the sole of the foot to trap the bouncing ball

(d) Gently push the ball forward

▶ **Pictures of Trapping a Bouncing Ball with the Inside of the Foot**

(a) Find the right position

(b) Trap the ball with the inside of the foot as soon as the ball hits the ground

(c) Gently push the ball to the intended position

▶ **Pictures of Trapping a Bouncing Ball with the Outside of the Foot**

(a) Find the right position

(b) Trap the ball with the outside of the foot as soon as the ball hits the ground

(c) Contact the ball with the outside of the foot

(d) Push the ball to the
intended position

▶ **Pictures of Trapping a Trap A Bouncing Ball between the Feet**
with Inside of the Foot

(a) Find the right position

(b) Watch the ball land

(c) Use the inside of the foot
to trap the ball

(d) Trap the ball from behind

(e) Possess the ball for deception

▶ **Practicing Trapping a Bouncing Ball**

1) Practice the bouncing trapping without a ball.

2) Self-toss the ball into the air and trap the ball with different parts of the foot as soon as it hits the ground (Diagram 48, 49, and 50).

Toss the Ball Upward

The Ball Drops Downward

Inside of Foot Trap
A Bouncing Ball

(Diagram 48)

Toss the Ball Upward

The Ball Drops Downward

Outside of Foot Trap
A Bouncing Ball

(Diagram 49)

Toss the Ball Upward

The Ball Drops Downward

Trap A Bouncing Ball
between the Feet

(Diagram 50)

3) Trap the bouncing ball tossed by a partner (Diagram 51).

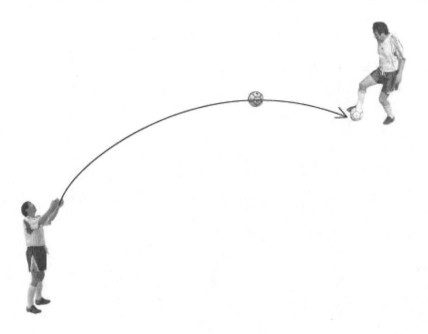

(Diagram 51)

4) Trap the bouncing ball kicked by a partner (Diagram 52).

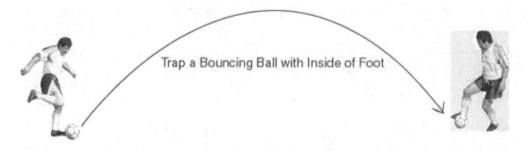

Trap a Bouncing Ball with Inside of Foot

(Diagram 52)

5) Trap an incoming bouncing ball while running (Diagram 53).

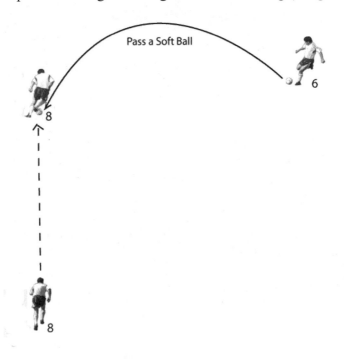

Pass a Soft Ball

(Diagram 53)

6) Trap an incoming bouncing ball with an opponent around (Diagram 54).

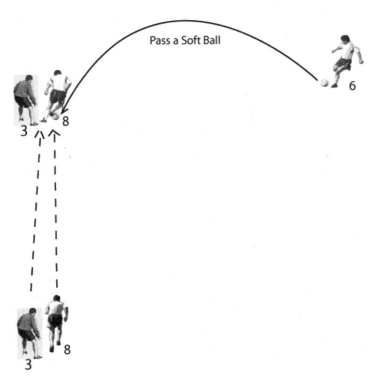

Pass a Soft Ball

(Diagram 54)

Chapter 4: Dribbling

Introduction

Dribbling is one of the most important and fundamental soccer skills. Every soccer player must execute dribbling well because it is intertwined with many other skills such as passing, defeating an opponent, adjusting the pace, implementing game strategy, scoring goals, and the like. Coaches must spend a great deal of time and effort to help their athletes master dribbling skills.

Depending on the purpose of dribbling, an athlete can use different dribbling techniques to accomplish his/her goals. There are four dribbling skills: (1) inside of the foot dribbling, (2) innerside of the instep dribbling, (3) instep dribbling, and (4) outside of the foot dribbling. The appropriate dribbling technique for a particular time and situation depends upon the position of the dribbler and the positions of the surrounding opponents. In addition to these basic dribbling skills, two critical elements of dribbling must be developed: (1) the ability to make a sudden change in direction and (2) the ability to make a sudden change of pace. Suddenly changing direction and pace while dribbling is the mark of a skilled soccer player because, when dribbling at a rapid speed, a player develops inertia - the force preventing him/her from changing direction and pace. Therefore, overcoming a strong inertia when dribbling must be the central focus of training in dribbling. The ability to effectively overcome inertia and suddenly change direction and pace while dribbling quickly can be a powerful weapon against an opposing team. Beyond that, dribbling is the pre-requisite for faking and beating opponents in competition.

In order to effectively make a sudden change of direction and pace, soccer players can use a variety of techniques. They can use different parts of the foot to contact the ball by lowering their center of gravity while dribbling. Also, the athletes must learn to execute various direction-changing techniques while dribbling. Once the athletes master these important techniques, they can enjoy every moment of play and build their self-confidence. The following section illustrates a variety of dribbling techniques.

▶ **Purpose of Dribbling**

The purpose of dribbling is to control the ball, initiate an attack, find the opportunity to score, assist teammates in attacking, create opportunities for teammates, penetrate the defense line, and so forth.

▶ **Technique of Dribbling**

- Relax the body, bend the knees, and push the ball to the intended position using different parts of the foot.

- Pay attention not only to the ball, but also to the peripheral surroundings to find the best position from which to pass or shoot.

- Keep the body relaxed.

▶ **Key Elements to Remember**

- Dribbling training should be emphasized constant changes in direction and pace so that the dribbler can learn to swiftly maneuver the ball.

▶ **Common Mistakes**

- Kicking the ball instead of pushing the ball forward.

- Kicking the ball too far.

- Always keep the eyes on the ball and do not pay attention to the surrounding areas.

Types of Dribbling

(1) Dribbling by Inside of Foot

▶ **Pictures of Inside of Foot Dribbling**

(a) Move the ball forward　　　　**(b) Assume the ready position before contacting**

(c) Point toe outward

(d) Contacts the ball with the inside of the foot

(e) Push the ball forward (don't kick)

(f) Move the ball forward

(2) Dribbling by Instep

▶ **Pictures of Instep Dribbling**

(a) Move the ball forward

(b) Point toe downward

(c) Push the ball forward with instep

(d) Control the ball within a reachable position

(e) Left instep pushes the ball forwards

(f) Contact the ball with the instep

(g) Move the ball forward

(3) Dribbling by Outside of Foot

▶ **Pictures of Outside of Foot Dribbling**

(a) Dribble the ball forward

(b) Point toe inward

(c) Outside of foot pushes the ball forward position

(d) Control the ball within a reachable

▶ Pictures of the Inside of Foot Cutting to the Opposite Direction

(a) Dribble the ball forward

(b) Ready to cut the ball

(c) Inside of foot cuts the ball backwards

(d) Turn body 180°

(e) Push the ball to the opposite foot

(f) Dribble the ball forwards

► **Pictures of the inside of foot cutting to the opposite direction-opposite view**

(a) Dribble the ball forward

(b) Ready to cut the ball

(c) Inside of foot cuts the ball backwards

(d) Dribble the ball forward

(a) Dribble the ball forward

(b) Outside of foot cuts the ball backward

(c) Turn body 180°

(d) Dribble the ball in the opposite direction

(e) Outside of foot pushes the ball forward

(f) Move forward

► Pictures of Cutting the Ball Backwards between the Feet

(a) Dribble the ball forward

(b) Turn the body backward

(c) Inside of foot cuts the ball backward

(d) Further turn the body

(e) Control the ball

(f) Dribble the ball in the opposite direction

► Pictures of Fake Swing by Same Foot Cutting the Ball Backward

(a) Move the ball forward

(b) Before cutting

(c) Fake swing upper-body
to the left direction

(d) Turning body backward

(e) Outside of foot cuts
the ball

(f) Dribble the ball in the
opposite direction

► **Pictures of Cross Ball Faking with Same Foot Cutting the Ball Backward**

(a) Push the ball forward

(b) Right foot crosses over the ball

(c) Turn the body 180°

(d) Outside of right foot cuts the ball in the opposite direction

(e) Move the ball forward

(f) Control the ball

▶ Pictures of Cross Ball Faking with Same Foot Cutting the Ball Background -Opposite View

(a) Push the ball forward

(b) Right foot crosses over the ball

(c) Turn the body 180°

(d) Outside of right foot cuts the ball in the opposite direction

(e) Move the ball forward

(f) Control the ball

(a) Move the ball forward the ball

(b) Before crossing over

(c) Right foot crosses over

(d) Turn the body 180°

(e) Turning the body

(f) Innerside of left foot cuts the ball backward

(g) Dribble in the opposite direction

▶ **Practice Dribbling**

1) Dribble following a Z path (Diagram 55).

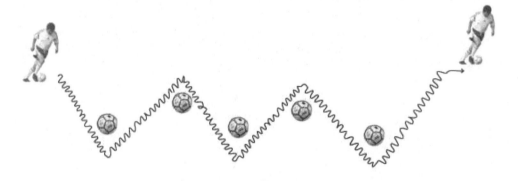

(Diagram 55)

2) Dribble within a fifteen-yard distance back and forth repeatedly (Diagram 56).

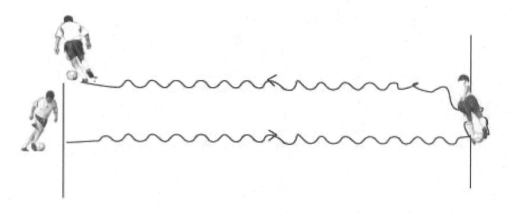

(Diagram 56)

3) Dribble while constantly changing directions (Diagram 57).

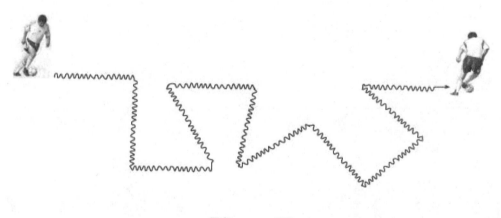

(Diagram 57)

4) Dribble around a circular path (Diagrams 58 and 59).

Note:dribble the ball with counter clockwise

(Diagram 58)

Note:dribble the ball with clockwise

(Diagram 59)

5) Dribble at varying paces (The high magnitude of the curves represents fast speed and vice versa) (Diagram 60).

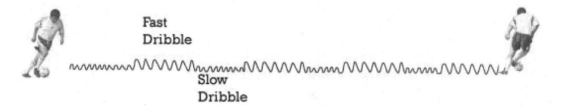

Fast
Dribble

Slow
Dribble

(Diagram 60)

6) Dribble with a sudden stop by making a 360° turn (Diagram 61).

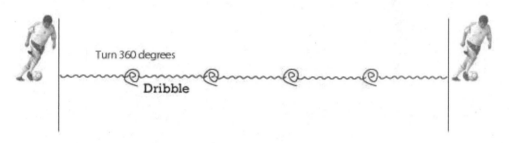

Turn 360 degrees

Dribble

(Diagram 61)

7) Dribble while constantly changing directions followed by a defend (Diagram 62).

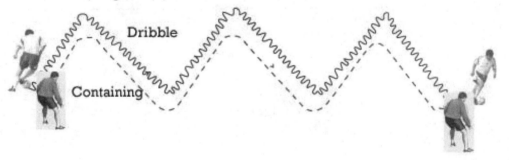

Dribble

Containing

(Diagram 62)

8) Dribble the ball back and forth to five different lines with varying the distances (Eight-yard distance between the two lines (Diagram 63).

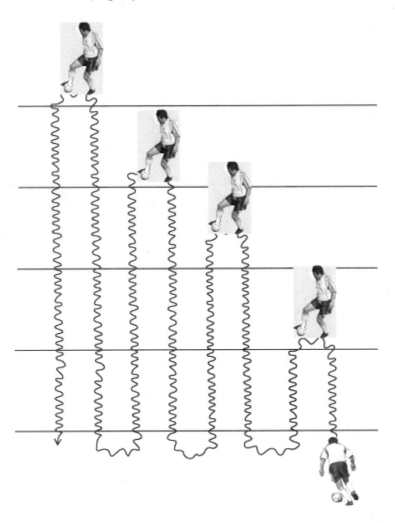

(Diagram 63)

9) Dribble the ball around the cones in a circular path (Diagram 64).

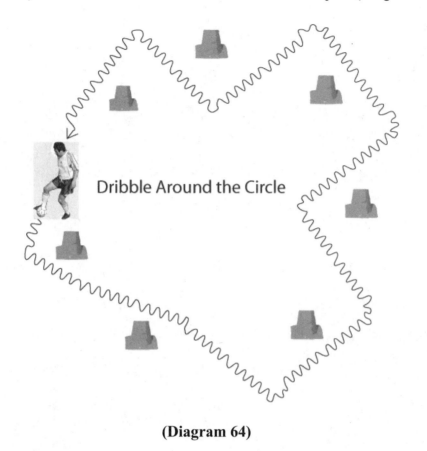

Dribble Around the Circle

(Diagram 64)

(10) Dribble the ball around the cones back and forth (Diagram 65).

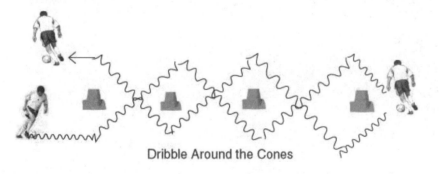

Dribble Around the Cones

(Diagram 65)

(11) Dribble the ball around the cones in a square path (Diagram 66).

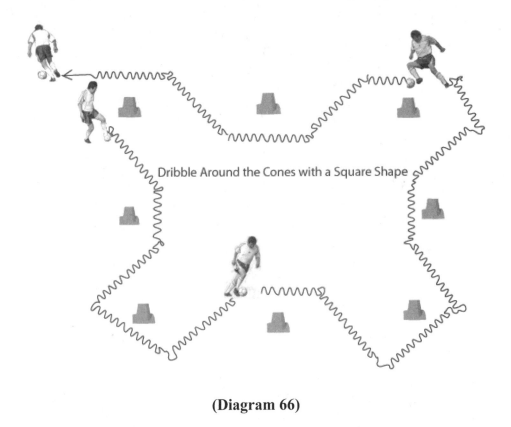

Dribble Around the Cones with a Square Shape

(Diagram 66)

(12) Randomly dribble the ball with a defender around (Diagram 67).

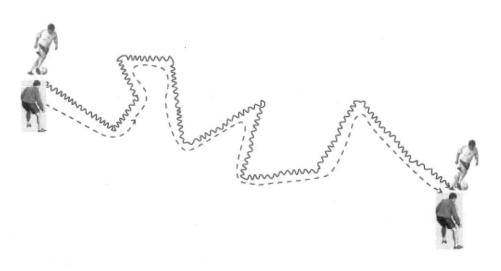

(Diagram 67)

(13) Ten to twelve players dribble within a designated box and neither the players nor the balls should be contacted one another (Diagram 68).

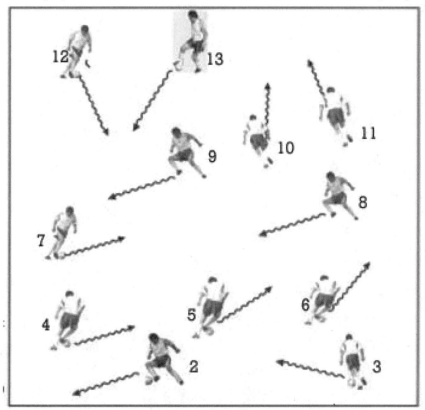

(Diagram 68)

(14) Half of the players stand stationary and another half of the players dribble within the designated box. No contact should be made between players or balls (Diagram 69).

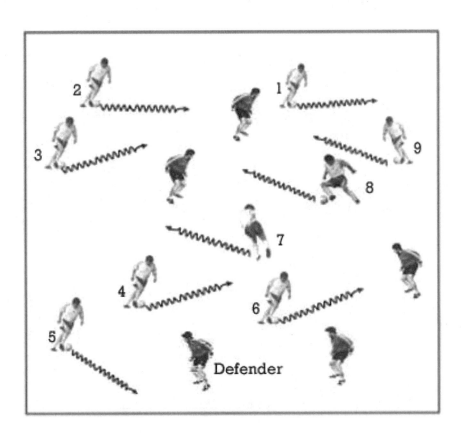

(Diagram 69)

(15) The coach gives signals to players who must dribble following the directions of coach is giving (Diagram 70).

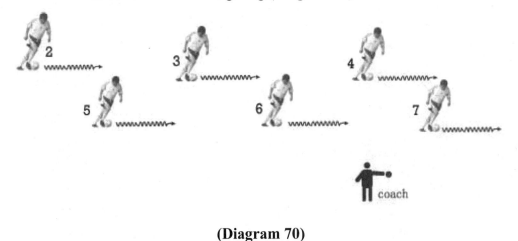

(Diagram 70)

Dribbling skills are very important because a soccer player must have swift and efficient dribbling skills in order to control the ball, make fake movements and beat an opponent. Thus, dribbling skills are the foundation for successfully executing many other soccer skills. Soccer athletes should learn various dribbling techniques including a variety of foot work, fake, and swing body movements. Suddenly changing pace and direction using various movements is central to successful and deceptive dribbling. Soccer learners must spend much time perfecting their dribbling skills so they can gain great advantage over opponents during competition. The following illustrations prevent various movements while dribbling for athletes to imitate and practice.

(4) Various Dribbling Movements for Changing Direction and Pace

Push the ball forward

Right foot crosses the ball

Left foot ready to cut the ball

Ready to turn the body

Outside of foot cutting

Inside of foot push

Making a fake movement

Sudden turn

Before turning the body

Inside of foot cutting

Outside of foot push

Inside of foot cutting

Instep push

Innerside of instep push

Dribbling

Right foot crosses the ball

Fake motion

Dribbling

Dribbling   **Dribbling**   **Ready to change direction**

Inside of foot cutting   **Change in direction**   **Outside of foot dribbling**

Ready to cut the ball

Change in direction

Change dribbling foot

Dribbling

Outside of foot dribble

Cross over ball while dribbling

Chapter 5: Faking and Beating Opponents

Introduction

Faking and beating the opponent are probably the most difficult soccer skills to learn because they are complex, must be completed in limited space while under intense pressure from the opposing players, and require precise timing, a sudden change of pace, and coordinated body movements. To successfully fake and beat the opponent, a soccer player must develop multiple abilities. Unfortunately, without a mastery of dribbling and faking skills, the athlete's chance for successfully scoring goals will be significantly minimized. All field players should develop these skills in competitive situations so that they can effectively transfer their practice skills to competition.

Opponent beating skills are (1) abilities to beat the opponent(s) with rapid speed, (2) abilities to use the simplest skill to beat the opponent(s), and (3) abilities to use the smallest space to beat the opponent(s). There are many different faking & opponent - beating skills and the learning sequence progresses from easy to difficult. Once all the faking and opponent-beating skills have been learned, the athlete in competition should use the simplest skill whenever possible to beat the opponent(s) because a simple skill is easy to perform and requires less energy and time to execute. Conversely, a fancy, complex, and time-consuming skill would be much less effective in competition. A rule of thumb every athlete should remember is, whenever possible, to use the simplest skill to beat an opponent in competition. In order to accomplish this goal, the athlete must master a variety of opponent-beating skills. Soccer players must make a great commitment to learn each of different skills for use in different situations during competition. The eleven opponent-beating skills illustrated below progress in sequence from easiest to most difficult. Each skill can be used when appropriate based on the game situation. It is highly recommended that every soccer player master all these skills effectively.

▶ **Purpose of Faking and Beating Opponent**

The purpose of faking and beating opponents is to allow a player to penetrate the defensive line in order to score, pass, or create opportunities for his/her teammates.

▶ **Technique of Faking and Beating Opponent**

- Keep the ball about one-and-a-half steps away from the defender so that it is close enough for the dribbler to beat the opponent, but too far for the defender to reach.

- The offender should approach the defender a slightly reduced speed, then suddenly accelerate and change dribbling direction in order to beat the defender.

- Proper timing when suddenly changing pace and direction is crucial to successfully beating the opponent.

▶ **Key Elements to Remember**

- Find the best timing to beat the opponent

- Change pace and direction while beating the opponent, moving from a relative slow pace to maximum speed.

▶ **Common Mistakes of Faking and Beating Opponent**:

- Hesitation.

- Timing error.

- Uncoordinated motions.

- Poor pacing.

Types of Opponent-Beating Techniques

(1) Speed Beating

Slowly approach the defender, then suddenly push the ball to one side as fast as possible.

▶ **Pictures of Speed Beating**

(a) Approaching the defender

(b) Suddenly speeding up and pushing the ball to the right

(c) Speeding up and beating the opponent

(d) Beating the opponent

(e) Possessing the ball

(2) Beating with Quick Touches between Two Feet

Approach the defender while touching the ball with the inside of the foot and immediately touching the ball with inside of the alternate foot; such actions make the defender ponder and hesitate. This hesitation allows the offender to beat the opponent quickly.

▶ **Pictures of Quick Touches between Two Feet**

(a)Touch the ball with the left foot

(b) Suddenly touch the ball with the right foot

(c) Touch the ball with the left foot again

(d) Use the left foot to beat the opponent

(2) Beating with Z Cutting with One Foot

The offender uses one foot to quickly push the ball to the left and right directions repeatedly. The zigzag motion is intended to confuse the defender, slowing down the defender's reaction time so that the offender can effectively beat the opponent.

▶ **Pictures of Z Cutting with One Foot**

(a) Right foot cuts the ball to the left

(b) Right foot pushes the ball to the right

(c) Right foot cuts the ball to the left again

(d) Left foot is ready to push the ball forward

(e) Left foot pushes the ball forward

(4) Beating with Single Swing Faking

One foot pretends to contact the ball, and the body moves in the same direction. Then, suddenly, the foot pushes the ball to the opposite direction to beat the defender.

▶ **Pictures of Single Swing Faking**

(a) Approach the opponent

(b) Swing the upper body to the left

(c) Suddenly swing the body to the right

(d) Push the ball to the right

(e) Move the ball forward

(5) Beating with Double Swing Faking

Same as single faking, but for this technique the body swings from left to right or right to left twice before pushing the ball to beat the defender.

▶ **Pictures of Double Swing Faking**

(a) Approach the opponent

(b) Swing body to the left

(c) Swing body to the right

(d) Swing body to the left again

(e) Swing body to the right again and push the ball to the right

(f) Speed up to beat the opponent

(6) Beating with Multiple Swing Faking

Same as double faking, but this technique requires that the body swing from left to right multiple times before pushing the ball to beat the defender.

(7) Beating with Cutting and Pushing the Ball with Alternate Foot

Move the ball to one direction, then suddenly cut the ball backwards using the inside of the alternate foot to quickly push the ball in the direction opposite its original trajectory to beat the defender.

▶ **Pictures of Cutting and Faking**

(a) Approach the opponent to the right back

(b) Right foot suddenly cuts the ball to left

(c) Cutting motion

(d) Body blocks the opponent and the left foot pushes the ball forward

(e) Speed up and beat the opponent

(f) Possess the ball

(8) Beating with Back Cutting and Pushing

Approach the defender's left side by suddenly cutting the ball behind the support foot, using the left foot to push the ball forward and the body to block the opponent.

(a) Approach the opponent

(b) Right foot in position to start cutting

(c) Start cutting

(d) Cut the ball to the left

(e) Reaching the ball again

(f) Left foot pushes the ball forward

(g) Beating the opponent

(h) Moving the ball forward

(9) Beating with Chipping an Air-Ball

Use the instep of the foot to suddenly lift the ball into the air and beat the defender.

▶ **Picture of Chipping an Air-Ball**

(a) Approach the opponent

(b) Ready to chip the ball

(c) Before chipping

(d) Chip the ball into the air

(e) Jump over to beat the opponent

(f) Possess the ball

(10) V Approach Beating

Push the ball to the right, then run past the defender on the left side. The ball and the dribbler from split to beat the defender.

▶ **Pictures of V Approach Beating**

(a) Approach the opponent

(b) Push the ball to the right

(c) Offender moves to the left to pass the opponent

(d) Speed up and passes the opponent

(e) Continue moving past the opponent

(f) Control the ball

(11) Beating Between the Feet:

If the defender's feet are too far apart, the offensive player should push the ball forward between the defender's feet.

▶ **Pictures of Beating Between the Feet**

(a) Approaching the opponent

(b) Getting closer

(c) Pushing the ball forward

(d) Pushing the ball between the opponent's feet

(e) Ball travels between the opponent's feet and the offender passes on the left

(f) Possessing the ball

(g) Controlling the ball.

► **Practicing Faking and Beating the Opponent**

• Practice Body Swing Motion.

(a) Swing body to the left

(b) Swing body to the right

(c) Swing body to the left again

(d) Swing body to the right again

- Practicing Faking Movement of Both Feet Crossing Over the Ball

(a) Push the ball forward

(b) Ready to fake

(c) Right foot crosses over the ball

(d) Fake body to the right

(e) Swing body to the left

(f) Left foot crosses over the ball

• Practicing Two Touches Faking

(a) Dribble the ball forward **(b) Swing body to the left** **(c) Inside of the foot touches the ball**

(d) Outside of the right foot immediately pushes the ball to right **(e) Change direction to right**

- Practicing One Touch Faking

(a) Swing body to the left

(b) Acting to touch the ball

(c) Suddenly touch the ball by outside of foot

- Practicing Cross Ball Faking

(a) Swing body to the left

(b) Cross left foot over the ball

(c) Outside of right foot pushes the ball to the right

(d) Push the ball to the right

▶ **Practicing Faking and Beating Opponents**

1) Practice one-on-one beating with a designated width from a large space to a small pace with a gradual process (Diagrams 71, 72, and 73).

Dribble

Approach the Offender

Beat the Opponent

(Diagram 71)

(Diagram 72)

(Diagram 73)

2) Practice one-on-two beating within a designated box (Diagram 74).

(Diagram 74)

3) Practice one-on-three beating within a designated box (Diagram 75).

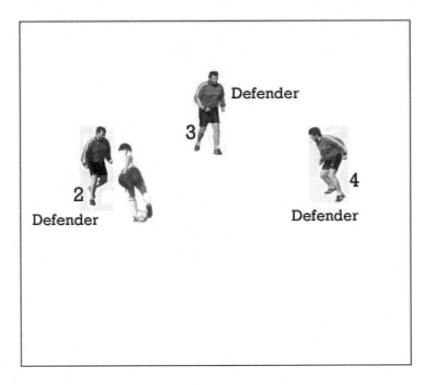

(Diagram 75)

4) Seven groups practice one-on-one beating within a designated box (Diagram 76).

(Diagram 76)

5) The coach passes a ball forward and two players fight to get the ball; whoever getting the ball becomes an offender and another player is the defender. The offender attempts to dribble and shoot the ball and the defender must disrupt the offender's attempt (Diagram 77).

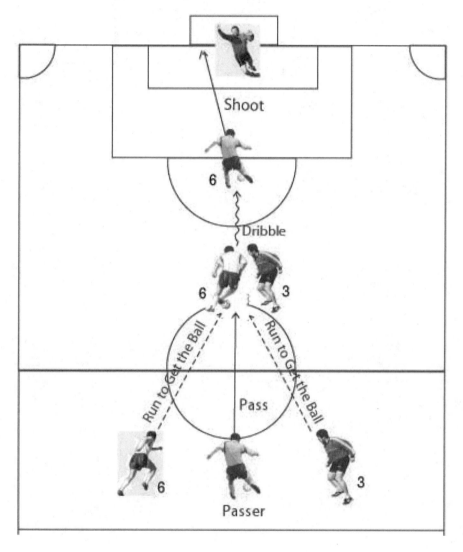

(Diagram 77)

6) The offender dribbles to beat a defender, then crosses the ball to center for the teammate's heading (Diagram 78).

(Diagram 78)

7) The coach passes the ball forward and both players fight for the ball. The winner becomes an offender to dribble and score a goal. The loser becomes a defender to tackle the ball (Diagram 79).

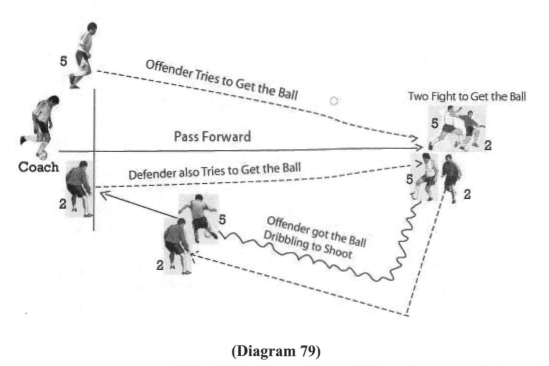

(Diagram 79)

8) Beat two opponents in the half of the field (Diagram 80).

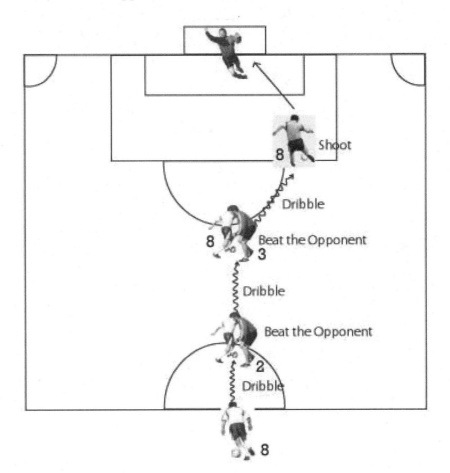

(Diagram 80)

9) Dribble with a Z path to beat multiple defenders to shoot (Diagram 81).

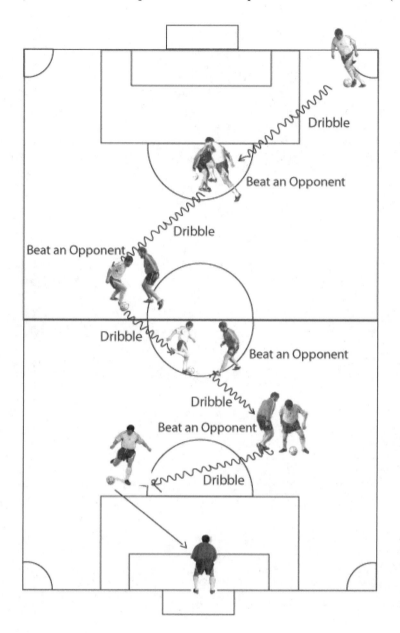

(Diagram 81)

10) Dribble straight ahead to beat multiple defenders to shoot (Diagram 82).

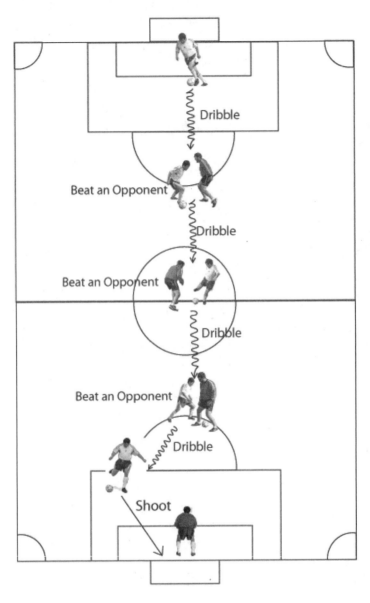

(Diagram 82)

Chapter 6: Tackling

Introduction

Soccer players will need to tackle the ball whenever their opponents have possession of it. Thus, effective tackling plays a vital role in determining which team controls the game during a competition. Unfortunately, many coaches have neglected to instruct their players in proper tackling techniques. Without well-mastered tackling skills, athletes will be at a great disadvantage in competition.

Tackling skills can be divided into face-to-face tackling, same direction tackling, and slide tackling, each of which has its own unique technical characteristics. Since 1974, the style of soccer being played has changed significantly. A popular strategy today is "the counter-attack approach," which means that both offensive and defensive players both must attack and defend regardless of their positions. Thus, not only are defenders responsible for playing defense, but offensive players must also act as defenders as soon as they lose possession of the ball. For example, the most popular soccer formations currently include: 4 - 4 - 2, 5 - 4 - 1, or 4 - 5 - 1. These formations demonstrate that in high-level competitions coaches put a great emphasis on the defense line to ensure their teams do not give up goals. Winning has become the second priority. In a soccer match, once a team gives up a goal it is a tremendous challenge to even the score. Therefore, the modern formations in soccer are designed to minimize the opponents' ability to score by strengthening the defense line. To achieve this objective, soccer coaches must focus on tackling and defensive practice in training their players. The following section lists the key elements of tackling skills; each of these technical components is vital to the development of soccer players' defensive skills. With dedicated and well-designed practice, athletes will significantly enhance their ability to tackle and their awareness of defensive principles.

▶ Purpose of Tackling

The purpose of tackling is to use legal play to take possession of the ball from an offender who is in control of it.

Types of Tackling Techniques

(1) Face to Face Tackling

▶ **Technique of Face to Face Tackling**

- Keep a containing position while watching the ball and quickly finding the best time to tackle.

- The tackle must be firm and fast using the inside of the foot to block and lift the ball across the offender's foot.

- Use the body to block the offensive player's movement in case of being unable to catch the ball.

▶ **Key Elements to Remember**

- Containing the offender and the ball.

- Time the tackle precisely.

- Tackle suddenly.

- Block the offender in case possession of the ball is lost.

▶ **Pictures of Face-to-Face Tackling**

(a) Approach the offender

(b) Prepare for tackle

(c) Quickly tackle the ball

(d) Inside of foot contacts and lifts the ball

(e) Lift the ball over the offender's foot

(f) Take possession of the ball

(2) Same Direction Tackling

▶ **Technique of Same Direction Tackling**

- Approach the ball alongside the opponent.

- Tackle the ball with a large final step, keeping a low center of gravity by bending the knees.

- Block the ball before kicking it rather than hastily contacting the ball first.

▶ **Key Elements to Remember**

- The final step should be large, jumping into the ball instead of running into it.

- <u>Keep a low center of gravity to increase the stability and balance while tackling.</u>

▶ **Pictures of Same Direction Tackling**

(a) Approach the ball

(b) Find the best position

(c) Position to block the opponent first

(d) Block the opponent with body and foot

(e) Control the ball

(3) Slide Tackling

▶ **Technique of Slide Tackling**

- Approach the ball in a position lateral to the offender by sliding one foot on the ground to push the ball away.

▶ **Pictures of Slide Tackling**

(a) Approach the ball from a lateral position

(b) Contact the ball with the sole of the foot

(c) Body leans backward

(d) Push the ball out of the offender's control

▶ **Practicing Tackling**

1) Practice the containing movement with an offender without using a ball (Diagram 83).

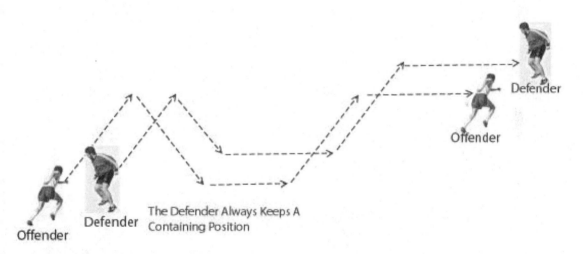

The Defender Always Keeps A Containing Position

(Diagram 83)

2) Practice the containing movement with an offender with a ball (Diagram 84).

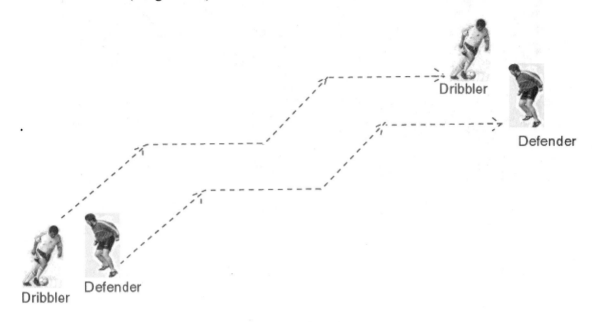

(Diagram 84)

3) Tackle a stationary ball from the same direction with an offender (Diagram 85).

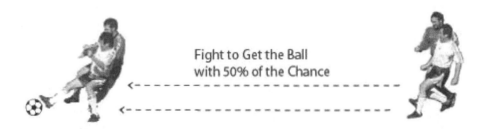

Fight to Get the Ball with 50% of the Chance

(Diagram 85)

4) Practice tackling with the face-to-face approach, the same-direction approach, and the sliding tackling approach (Diagram 86).

Run to Get the Ball   Run to Get the Ball

(Diagram 86)

5) Two against three within a designated box (Diagram 87).

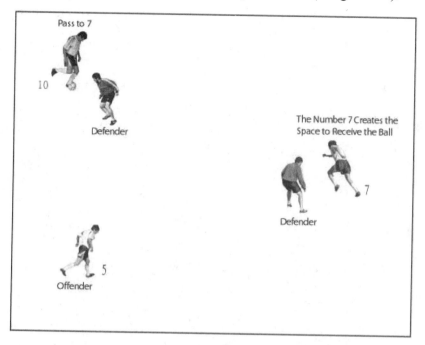

(Diagram 87)

6) Five against five within a designated box (Diagram 88).

(Diagram 88)

7) Fight for a ball by tackling another player; whoever gets the ball first becomes the offender for shooting. Another player becomes a defender to tackle the ball (Diagram 89).

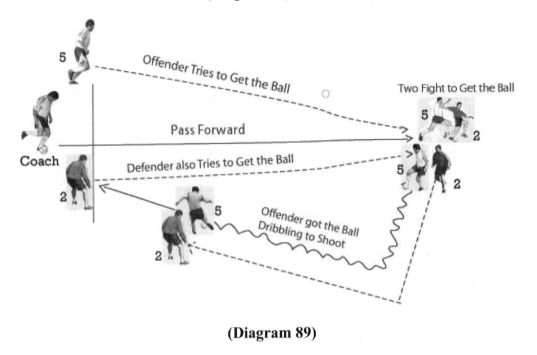

(Diagram 89)

8) Two players tackle the ball to shoot (Diagram 90).

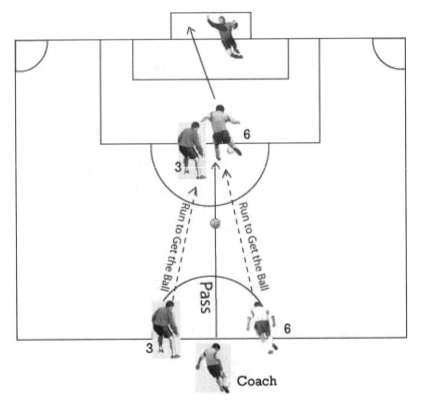

(Diagram 90)

9) An offender dribbles the ball to shoot, and a defender tries to tackle the ball (Diagram 91).

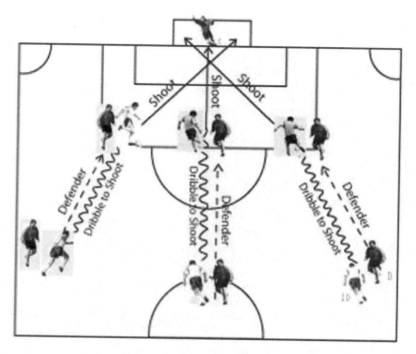

(Diagram 91)

Chapter 7: Heading

Introduction

The soccer player's head is considered a third foot due to its frequent use and effectiveness in scoring goals. When a ball is in the air during competition, both teams fight for an air-ball by heading. Heading can be used for passing, scoring, or clearing the ball for defensive play. Every player on the field uses heading to accomplish different goals. Three objectives of heading are accuracy, speed, and distance. For scoring, heading should be executed with great accuracy and speed. For passing, heading should be performed in a precise fashion for accuracy and proper force. For clearing the ball as a defensive play, heading is required for maximum distance.

There are three different types of heading: (1) heading while standing on the ground, (2) heading while jumping into the air for a high ball, and (3) heading while diving for a low ball (This skill is not introduced here). The first two heading techniques are similar; the only difference is the ball is at different heights. The third type of heading requires a high degree of athletic ability because it demands swift skills, precise timing, and extreme flexibility. Once players master these heading skills, they are in a good position to dominate the air-ball.

A common problem in learning heading is that many novice players are afraid to use their heads to hit the ball. This fear can significantly hamper their learning outcomes. Thus, coaches must show their athletes that a soccer ball will not hurt their heads if heading is performed properly. They should also emphasize that players must keep their eyes open while using their foreheads to contact the ball. With a comprehensive understanding of these major components of the skill, students should be able to eliminate their fear of heading.

▶ **Purpose of Heading**

The purpose of heading is scoring, passing, and defending.

▶ **Technique of Heading**

- Keep feet apart.

- Keep neck tight and straight.

- Use abdominal muscles to generate movement at the waist while hitting the ball with the forehead.

► **Key Elements to Remember**

- Major force of heading comes from waist movement (use abdominal muscles instead of neck movement).

- Always keep eyes open and both hands up while heading.

► **Common Mistakes**

- Moving the neck in a small range of motion.

- Hitting the ball with the top of the head.
  Types of Heading

(1) Pictures of Standing Heading

(a) Get in the ready position by moving the body backward

(b) Contact the ball with the forehead

(c) Swing the body forward with quick motion

(2) Pictures of Jump-Heading

(a) Jump into the air to head a high ball

(b) Use forehead to hit the ball

(c) Follow through Motion

(3) Pictures of Jump Heading the Ball to a Different Direction

(a) Prepare to jump

(b) Jump into the air to head the ball

(c) Head the ball out

(d) Successful heading

(e) Landing with good balance

▶ **Practicing Heading**

1) Practice heading without the ball.

2) Practice balancing a ball on the head (Diagram 91).

3) Self-head a ball into the air repeatedly (Diagram 92).

(Diagram 91)   **(Diagram 92)**

4) Head a ball tossed by a partner (Diagram 93).

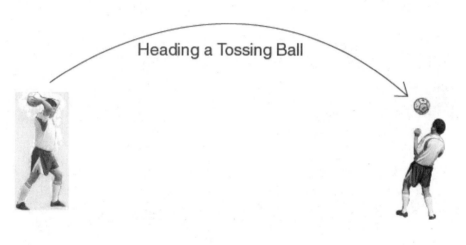

Heading a Tossing Ball

(Diagram 93)

5) Two players head the ball back and forth repeatedly (Diagram 94).

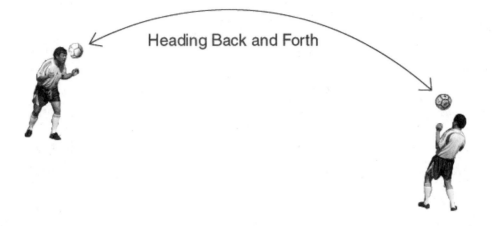

(Diagram 94)

6) Head a ball kicked by a partner (Diagram 95).

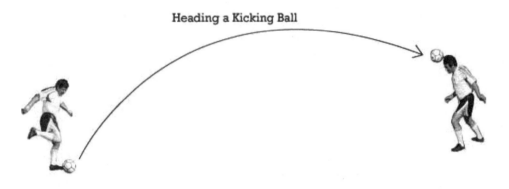

(Diagram 95)

7) Jump head a ball kicked by a partner (Diagram 96).

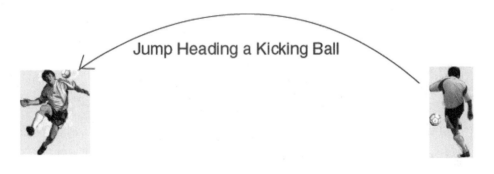

(Diagram 96)

8) Three players head among themselves in a triangle position (Diagram 97).

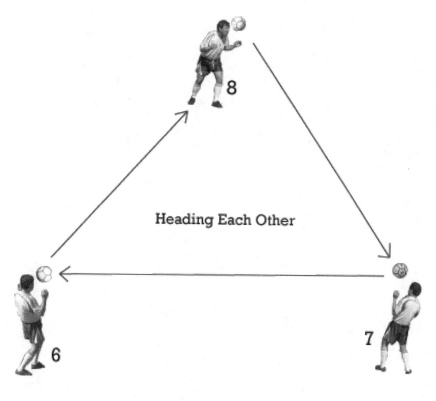

(Diagram 97)

9) Six players head among themselves in a circular position (Diagram 98).

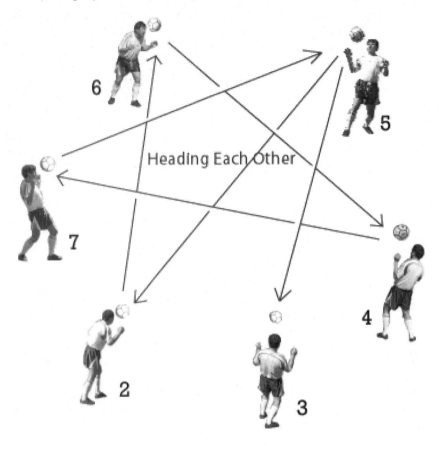

Heading Each Other

(Diagram 98)

10) Players 2, 3, and 4 stand in a line facing players 5, 6, 7, who stand approximately ten yards away. Player 2 passes a ball to player 5; Player 2 immediately runs forward to stand behind player 7. As soon as player 5 sees the ball come, he/she passes it to player 3. Both groups pass the ball back and forth and repeat the process (Diagram 99).

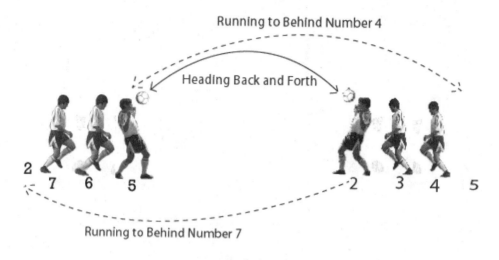

(Diagram 99)

11) Head a tossed ball to score a goal (Diagram 100).

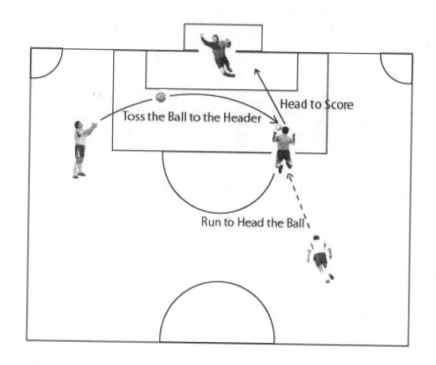

(Diagram 100)

12) Jump head a long distance ball kicked by a partner (Diagram 101).

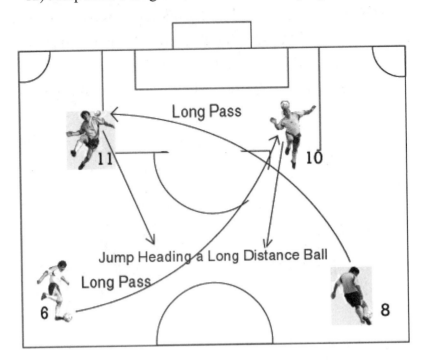

(Diagram 101)

13) Head a corner kick to score a goal (Diagram 102).

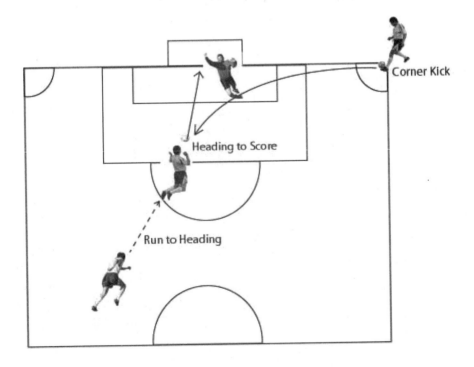

(Diagram 102)

14) Head a ball passed by a teammate (Diagram 103).

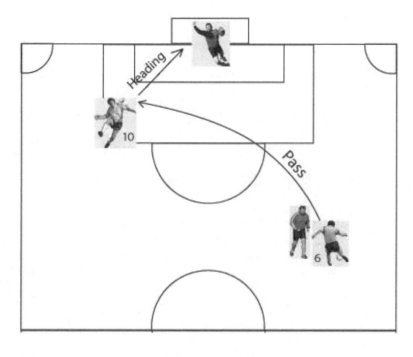

(Diagram 103)

15) Jump heading a corner kick to score a goal (Diagram 104).

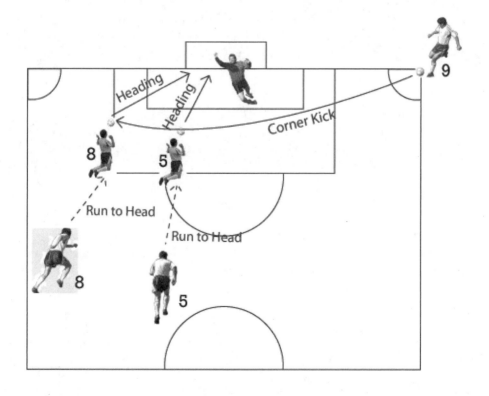

(Diagram 104)

16) Jump head a corner kick to score a goal with opponents around (Diagram 105).

Corner Kick

(Diagram 105)

Chapter 8: Throwing-In

Introduction

When a ball is kicked across the sideline, the opposing team has to re-start the game by throwing-in the ball. Usually, the player who engages in throwing-in must have great muscular strength in the upper arms in order to throw the ball to a designated place on the field, which may be a long distance. Especially when throwing-in occurs near the endline, a forceful throw can project the ball to the center of the goal area just like a corner kick, putting the opposition at great risk of losing the goal. Beyond that, throwing-in requires the field players and thrower to work together to create an opportunity on attack. Even though the technique of throwing-in is relatively simple, the thrower needs to have sufficient muscular strength and be able to effectively collaborate with the field players.

▶ **Purpose of Throwing-In**

Throwing-in is the only way to re-start the game when the ball crosses a sideline, and it creates the opportunity for thrower's teammates to attack.

▶ **Technique of Throwing-In**

- The thrower's feet remain on the ground, either in a stationary position or a sliding motion throughout the entire process.

- Use two hands to hold the ball.

- Placing the ball behind the head and move it above the head with a continuous motion.

- Throwing the ball to an intended teammate or position.

▶ **Key Elements to Remember**

- <u>Always keep both feet on the ground.</u>

- <u>Throw the ball using a continuous motion.</u>

▶ **Pictures of Throwing**

(a) Two hands hold the ball behind the head

(b) Both feet remain on the ground

(c) Throw the ball with a continuous motion

(d) Throw the ball over the top of the head

(e) Throw the ball

(f) Follow through

► **Practicing Throwing-In**

1) Throw a ball to each other (Diagram 106).

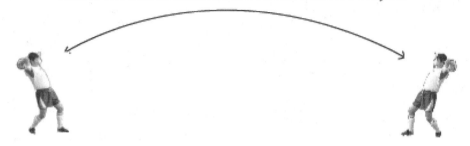

(Diagram 106)

2) Throw a ball as far as possible.

3) Throw a ball to a running teammate (Diagram 107).

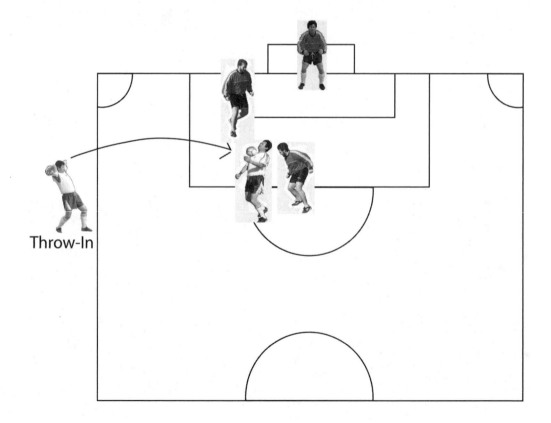

(Diagram 107)

Chapter 9: Goalie Skills

Introduction

Soccer goalie has unique responsibilities that are entirely different from those of the field players. A goalie can use his/her hands, arms and every other part of the body to contact the ball in order to prevent the opponent from scoring within the penalty box. The player who serves as goalie must possess certain basic talents/abilities: (1) fast reaction time, (2) swiftness of eye and hand coordination, (3) extreme jumping ability, (4) body flexibility, (5) great sense and perception of position awareness, (6) quick and wise decision-making skills, and (7) quickness of muscular movement. Since many of these talents are genetically determined, it is crucial to select the right person to be goalie. Without these innate abilities and the proper training, a goalie will not be successful and effective.

The goalie's skills include catching the ball at different levels, punching the ball for clearance, save the ball by diving, kicking the ball for passing or clearing the ball, and so forth. Besides using his/her hands, the goalie must also learn to kick the ball if needed. A goalie's kicking skills are similar to those of the field players. The following are the fundamental skills required for goalies.

Types of Goalie Skills

(1) Catching a Ground Ball

▶ **Technique One: Catching a Ground Ball with Bended Knees**

- Place one leg in a lateral position as a second protection in case the ball is not caught with the hands.

► **Pictures of Catching a Ground Ball with Bended Knees**

(a) Find the best position

(b) Assume the ready position

(c) Before catching the ball

(d) Contacting the ball

(e) Catching the ball

(f) Possessing the ball

(g) Controlling the ball

▶ **Technique of Catching a Ground Ball with Extended Knees**

- Both hands face upwards to catch the ball with feet a short distance apart less than a ball's width.

▶ **Pictures of Catching a Ground Ball with Extended Knees**

(a) Find the best position

(b) Bend at the waist keeping the hands up

(c) Catch the ball

(d) Possess the ball safely

(2) Catching a Low Air-Ball

    ▶ **Technique of Catching a Low Air-Ball**

        • Both hands face upwards to catch the ball gently by bending the elbow.

    ▶ **Pictures of Catching a Low Air-Ball**

(a) Extend both arms with hands face up

(b) Catch the ball smoothly

(c) Protect the ball   **(d) Control the ball**

(3) Catching an Overhead Air-Ball

▶ **Technique of Catching an Overhead Air-Ball**

- Both hands facing forward, side by side, to catch the ball.

(a) Predict the position of the incoming ball

(b) Extend arms with hands forward to catch the ball

(c) Bring the ball back

(d) Hold the ball safely

(4) Catching a High Air-Ball

▶ **Technique of Catching a High Air-Ball**

- Predict the direction of the incoming high ball.

- Jump into the air to catch the ball.

- Two hands face forward with a side-by-side position to catch the ball.

- Bring he ball down to hold a safe position.

▶ **Pictures of Catching a High Air-Ball**

(a) Predict the position of the incoming ball

(b) Jump into the air and catch the ball

(c) Bring the ball back

(d) Hold the ball safely

(5) Catching an Air-Ball with Two Hands at Either Side

▶ **Technique of Catching an Air-Ball with Two Hands at Either Side**

• Extend both arms with hands facing forward.

• Bring the ball back to the body as soon as it is caught.

▶ **Pictures of Catching an Air-Ball with Two Hands at Either Side**

(a) Jump laterally to catch the ball with both hands

(b) Bring the ball back toward the body

(c) Control the ball

(6) Catching an Air-Ball with One Hand at Either Side

   ▶ **Technique of Catching an Air-Ball with One Hand at Either Side**

      • Extend one arm to with the hand facing forward.

      • Block the ball and bring it back to the body as soon as it is caught.

   ▶ **Pictures of Catching an Air-Ball with One Hand at Either Side**

(a) Catch the ball to one side with
one hand

(b) Bring the ball back toward the body

| (c) Possess the ball | (d) Control the ball |

(7) Diving to Catch an Air-Ball at Either Side

▶ **Technique of Diving to Catch an Air-Ball at Either Side**

• Dive with one shoulder landing on the ground first, followed by body, hip, upper leg, and lower leg sequentially.

▶ **Picture of Diving to Catch an Air-Ball at Either Side**

Catching an air-ball at Either Side

(8) Punching the Ball with the Fists

   ▶ **Technique of Punching the Ball with the Fists**

      ● Predict the position of a high incoming air-ball.

      ● Jump into the air as high as possible to punch the ball with one fist or both fists.

   ▶ **Pictures of Punching the Ball with the Fists**

(a) Ready to jump

(b) Jump into the Air

(c) Punching the ball with both fists

(d) Punching the ball into the air

Punching the ball with one fist

(9) Kick a Bouncing Ball

▶ **Technique of Kicking a Bouncing Ball**

- Hold the ball with one hand to make a large and final stride.

- Drop the ball to an intended position.

- Swing the kicking foot as fast as possible.

- Contact the ball with the instep of the foot.

▶ **Pictures of Kick a Bouncing Ball**

(a) Ready to drop the ball

(b) Drop the ball

(c) Ready to kick

(d) Swinging motion

(e) Contact the ball

(f) Kick the ball out

Chapter 10: Ball Control Skills

Introduction

Learning ball control skills is one of the major stages in soccer skill progression because soccer players should be able to manipulate the ball as swiftly with their feet as they can with their hands. Ball control practice is the most effective way to help athletes become familiar with the ball and maneuver it wherever and whenever they wish. The patterns of ball control practice may seem unrelated to soccer competition, but these types of practice can significantly enhance an athlete's ability to control the ball.

Learning ball control skills can be achieved at many different settings and times because the requirements of space and time are very flexible. For example, an athlete can practice ball control skills in a living room, driveway, or soccer field. Players can practice two minutes, ten minutes, or half an hour whenever they have time to practice. Once athletes have learned these ball control skills, their competence playing soccer game will be immensely enhanced.

Types of Ball Control Skills

(1) Juggling: Juggling the ball by head, thigh, instep, inside and outside of the feet. More advanced athletes can juggle the ball with their shoulders and heels.

> ▶ **Purpose of Juggling:**
>
> To be familiar with the reactions of the ball.
>
> *Please see photos on following page.*

► **Types of Juggling:**

1) Juggling with the Instep

(a) Juggle the ball with instep of the right foot

(b) Switch to left foot

(c) Left foot juggles

2) Juggling with the Inside of the Foot

(a) Inside of foot contacts the ball

(b) Juggle the ball upwards

(c) Juggle the ball repeatedly

3) Juggling with the Outside of the Foot

(a) Outside of foot contacts the ball

(b) Juggle the ball upwards

(c) Juggle the ball repeatedly

4) Juggling with the Thigh

(a) Thigh contacts the ball

(b) Thigh juggling

5) Juggling with the Head

(a) Hit the ball upward

(b) Contact the ball with the forehead

(c) Repeatedly head the ball

(2) Instep Catching the Ball

(a) Raise a foot to receive the ball

(b) Instep catches the ball

(c) Foot moves downwards   **(d) Instep catches the ball**

(3) Balancing the Ball on the Head

Balance the Ball on Forehead

(4) Instep Pushing and Sole of the Foot Pulling

(a) Sole of foot pulls the ball backward

(b) Push the ball forward with instep

(c) Push the ball forward

(d) Pull the ball backward again

(e) Instep pushes the ball forward again

(5) Inside of the Foot Pushing and Sole of the Foot Pulling

(a) Sole of the foot pulls the ball backward

(b) Push the ball forward

(c) Push the Ball Forward with inside of the foot

(d) Pull the ball backward again

(e) Inside of the foot pushes the ball forward again

(f) Push the ball forward

(6) Outside of the Foot Pushing and Sole of the Foot Pulling

(a) Sole of the foot pulls
the ball backward

(b) Push the ball forward

(c) Push the ball forward
with outside of the foot

(d) Sole of the foot pulls
the ball backward

(e) Push the ball forward

(f) Push the ball forward
with outside of the foot

(7) Pulling and Pushing the Ball with 90 Degree Change of the Direction

(a) Dribble the ball forward

(b) Ready position to pull the ball

(c) Sole of the foot pulls the ball backward

(d) Inside of the foot pushes the ball to 90° direction

(e) Dribble the Ball Forward

(8) Two Quick Touches with the Inside and the Outside of the Same Foot

(a) Right foot is moving to foot contact the right side of the ball

(b) Inside of the right foot contacts the right side of the ball

(c) The outside of the right contacts the left side of the ball

(9) Rolling the Ball to the Opposite Position Alternatively

(a) Sole of the right foot pulls the ball to the left

(b) Pulling the ball to the left

(c) Left foot ready to pull

(d) Sole of the left foot pulls the ball to the right

(e) Pulling the ball to the right

(10) Outside of the Foot Pushes the Ball to Both Directions

(a) Outside of the right foot pushes the ball to the right

(b) Switch to use the left foot

(c) Outside of the left foot pushes the ball to the left

(d) Switch to use the left foot

(e) Outside of the right foot pushes the ball to the right

(f) Moving the ball to the right

(g) Switch to use the left foot

(h) Outside of the left foot pushes he ball to the left

Chapter 11: Basic Tactics and Strategies

Introduction

In a soccer competition, athletes use various basic tactics to engage in collaborative work to accomplish immediate goals. For example, soccer athletes most often use the two against one (2 to 1) tactic to beat an opponent and possession of the ball. There are many different ways to implement two against one tactics; once players learn these collaborative tactics, their strength as a team is significantly enhanced. This short chapter introduces some of the most fundamental tactics; yet, these tactics have proven to be the most effective, and most used, in soccer competition.

Basic Tactics of Passing

(1) Two to One Passing (Two against One)

- **Cross Passing and Straight Running** - Players 6 and 7 keep seven yards apart, facing the same direction and pass a ball to each other while slowly running straight ahead (Diagram 108).

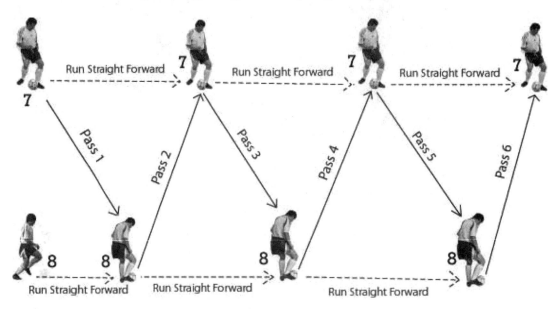

(Diagram 108)

- **Straight Passing and Cross Running** - Player 6 passes the ball straight to player 7 who runs from the opposite side of the position. Meanwhile, As soon as player 6 passed the ball to player 7, player 6 runs to the opposite side to receive the ball from player 7. Two players repeat the process in order to practice the inside of foot pass (Diagram 109).

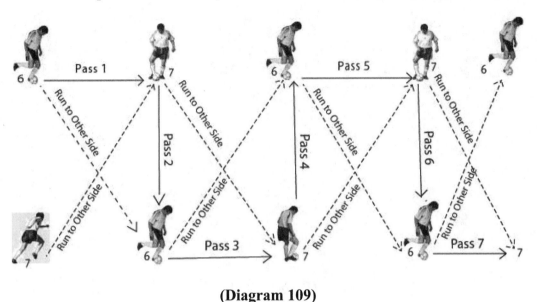

(Diagram 109)

- **Opposite Direction Passing** - Player 5 dribbles the ball to the opposite position and player 6 runs to another side to receive the ball passed by player 5. Player 6 will repeat the same process as player 5 did. Consistently, player 5 will repeat the process as player 6 just did (Diagram 110).

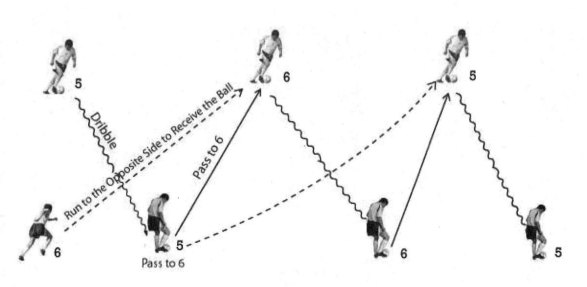

(Diagram 110)

- **Wall Passing** - Player 5 passes the ball to player 6 and player 5 immediately runs forward on the right side or left side to receive the ball from player 6 and dribble the ball forward to bypass the defender (Diagram 111).

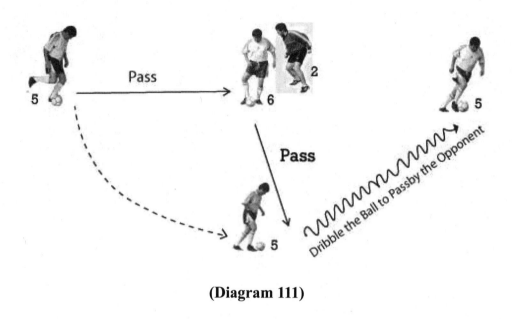

(Diagram 111)

- **Chip over Head Passing** - Player 4 chips the ball over the defender's head and player 6 runs over to receive the ball passed by player 4 (Diagram 112).

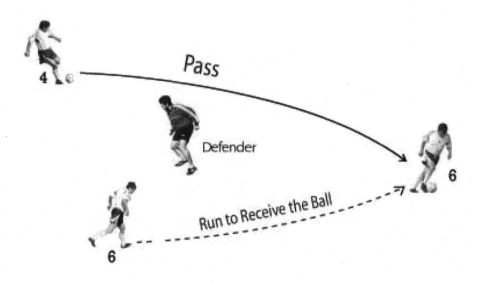

(Diagram 112)

- **Triangle Dribbling and Back Passing** - Player 5 dribbles the ball to the center and back-passes it to player 6 who runs behind player 5. After passed the ball, player 5 runs to opposite side of the position. After receiving the ball from player 5, player 6 dribbles the ball forward. After that, player 6 repeats the same process as player 5 just did and vice versa for player 5 (Diagram 113).

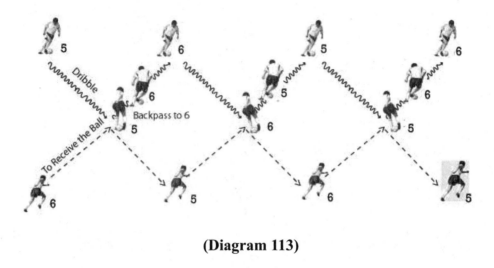

(Diagram 113)

- **Triangle Dribbling and Opposite Passing** - Player 6 dribbles the ball to the center and player 8 runs over behind player 6. Player 6 passes the ball to player 8 and continuously runs forward. Player 8 will next execute player 6's process and vice versa for player 6 (Diagram 114).

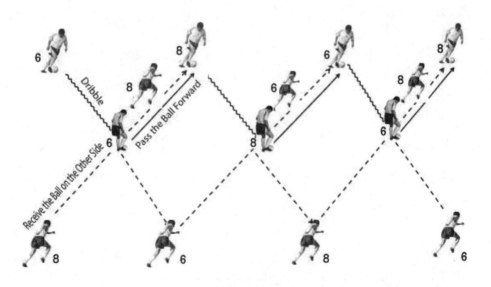

(Diagram 114)

(2) Three to One Passing – Three players pass the ball each other and a defender tries to get the ball from them (Diagram 115).

(Diagram 115)

(3) Three to Two Passing – Three players pass the ball each other and two defenders try to get the ball from them (Diagram 116).

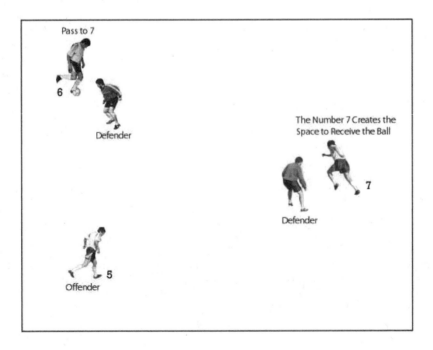

(Diagram 116)

(4) Four to Two Passing - Four players pass the ball each other and two defenders try to get the ball from them (Diagram 117).

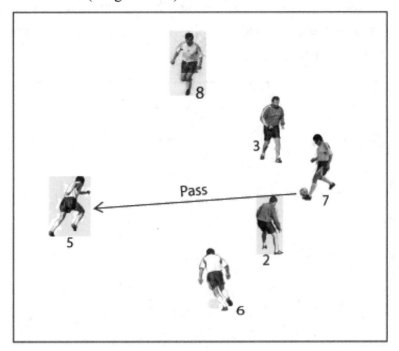

(Diagram 117)

(5) Five to Five Approach - Five players pass each other and five defenders try to get the ball from them (Diagram 118).

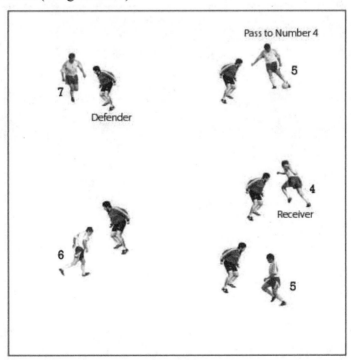

(Diagram 118)

(6) Down to the Endline Cross-over Passing

(a). Player 8 dribbles the ball toward the end-line and makes a cross-over pass to the center and then player 10 or player 11 shoots or heads the ball to score (Diagrams 119).

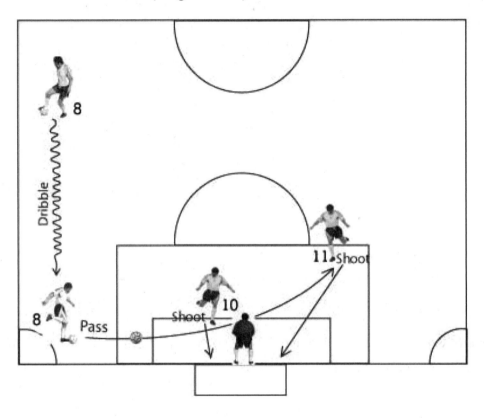

(Diagram 119)

(b). Player 10 dribbles the ball toward the end-line and makes a cross-over
pass to the center and then player 11 shoots or heads the ball to score
(Diagrams 120).

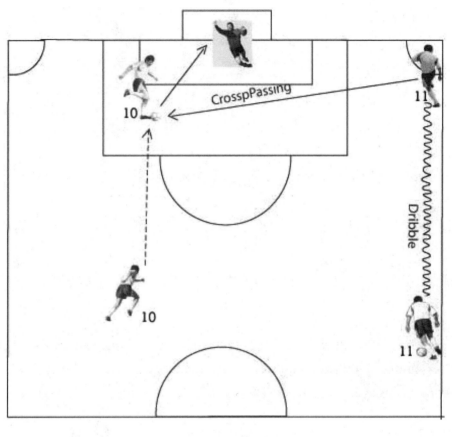

(Diagram 120)

(7) Dribbling with Opposite Passing - Player 6 dribbles the ball to the opposite side and player 8 also runs to the opposite side. Player 6 makes a cross pass to player 8 who can either shoot or dribble the ball (Diagram 121).

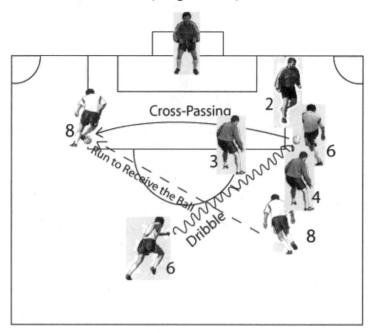

(Diagram 121)

(8) Back-Passing Play - Player 8 dribbles the ball to the end line and draws several defenders around him/her, and then passes the ball backward to player 6, who makes a cross-pass to player 10 to shoot (Diagram 122).

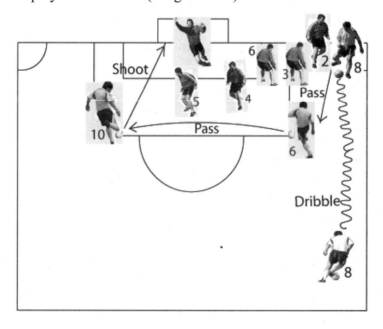

(Diagram 122)

(9) Deceptive Play - Player 6 dribbles the ball forward and player 8 runs to left side. As soon as player 8 reaches beside player 6 who immediately makes a pass between-feet to player 8 who shoots the ball (Diagram 123).

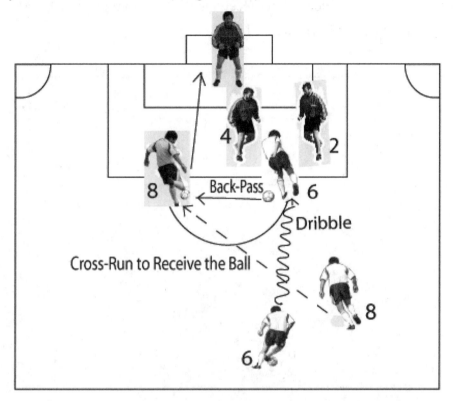

(Diagram 123)

Strategies for Starting a Game

(1) Back Pass Strategy: Player 11 passes the ball to player 10 who passes the ball to player 6 who is the midfielder. After receiving the ball from player 10, player 6 passes the ball to player 10 (Diagram 124).

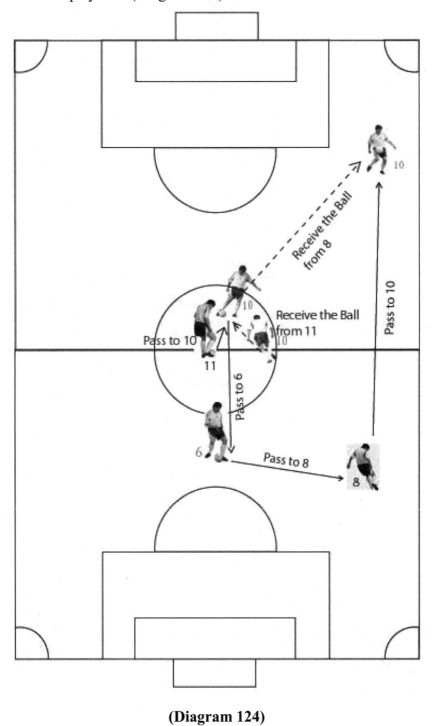

(Diagram 124)

(2) Short Pass Strategy: Player 10 passes the ball to player 11 who passes the ball back to player 10 who passes the ball back to player 11 (Diagram 125).

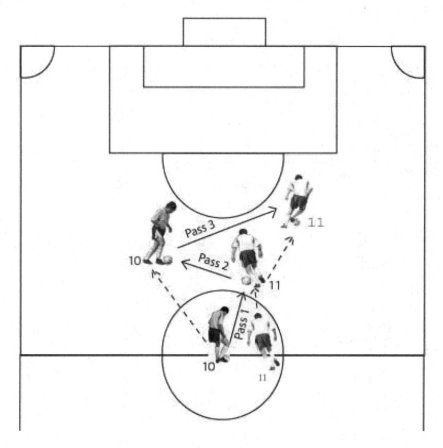

(Diagram 125)

(3) Long Pass Strategy: Player 10 makes a short pass to player 11 and player 11 immediately sprint to the left corner of the end line to receive a long pass from player 11 (Diagram 126).

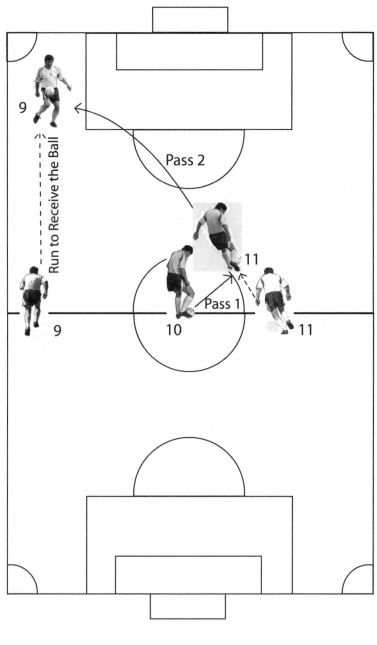

(Diagram 126)

Strategies for a Corner Kick

(1) Directly kick the ball to the center of the goal area for a teammate's heading to score (diagram 127).

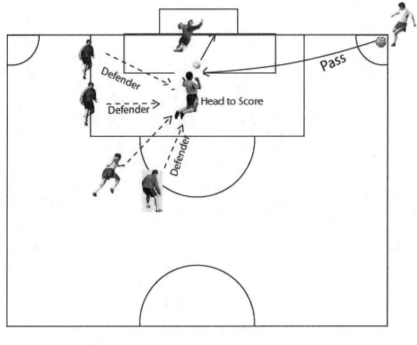

(Diagram 127)

(2) Player 6 passes the ball to player 5 who passes the ball back to player 6. As soon as receiving the ball, player 6 cross-passes the ball to player 10 to score (Diagram 128).

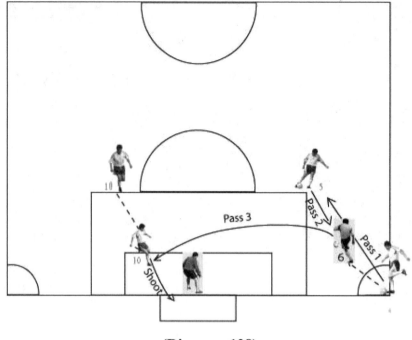

(Diagram 128)

(3) The corner kicker kicks the ball to directly score a goal (Diagram 129).

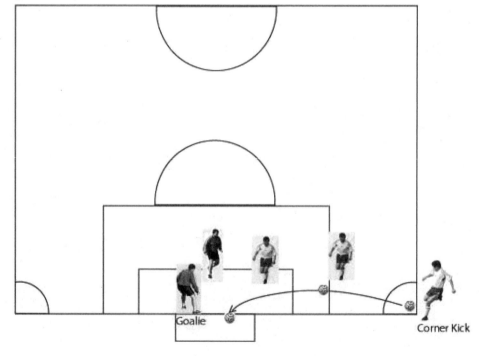

(Diagram 129)

(4) Player 6 passes the ball to player 7 who passes it to player 8 to score (Diagram 130).

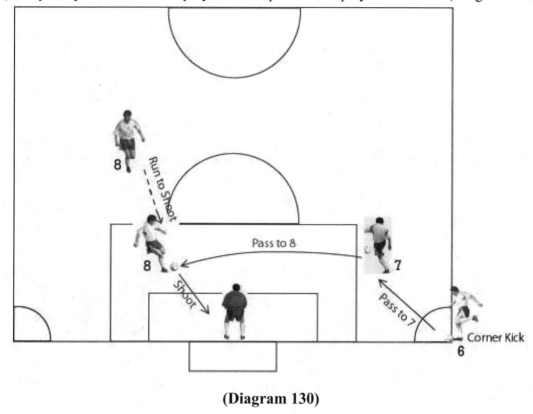

(Diagram 130)

(5) Directly passes the ball to the goal area for shooting (Diagram 131).

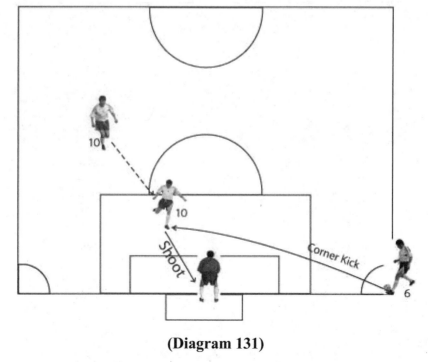

(Diagram 131)

(6) Kick a high ball for a teammate's heading to score (Diagram 132).

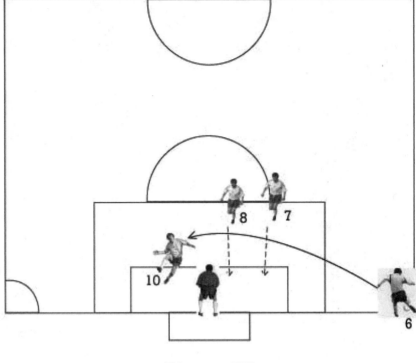

(Diagram 132)

Strategies for Direct or Indirect Free Kick

(1) The kicker passes the ball to the opposite side of the area, player 9 receives the ball to shoot (Diagram 133).

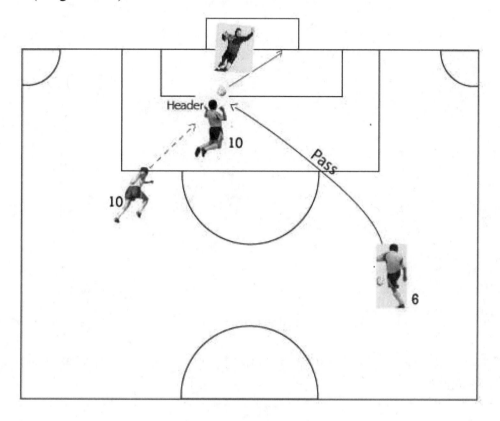

(Diagram 133)

(2) Players 7 and 8 both make a fake run and player 10 shoots the ball to a goal directly. This type free kick can disrupt the defenders' attention (Diagram 134).

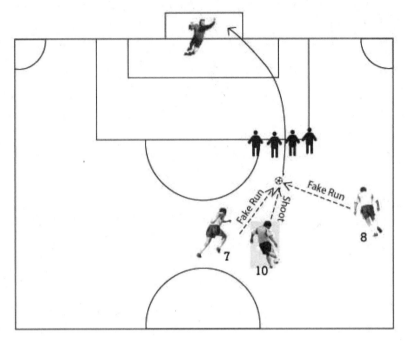

(Diagram 134)

(3) Player 6 chips the ball to behind the wall and player 10 receives the ball to shoot (Diagram 135).

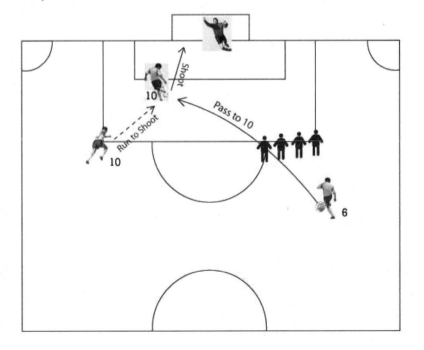

(Diagram 135)

(4) Make a curve ball kick to score a goal directly (Diagram 136).

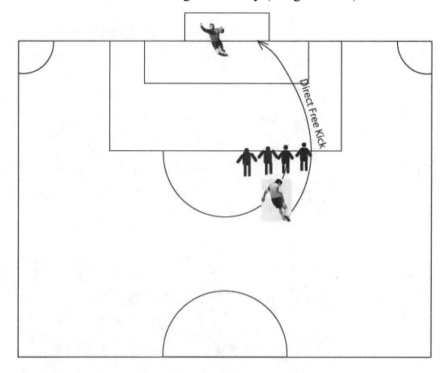

Direct Free Kick

(Diagram 136)

Strategies for a Goal Kick

(1) The goalie passes the ball to player 3, who passes the ball back to the goalie, who catch the ball with his/her hands and then punts the ball to the designated area. (Diagram 137).

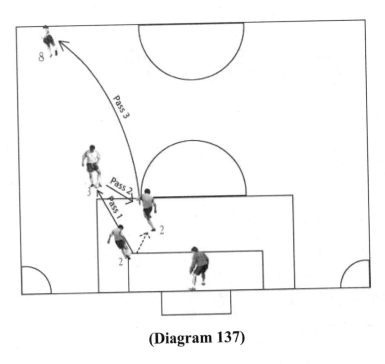

(Diagram 137)

(2) Player 4 passes a long ball to player 7 or player 8, and the ball should be distributed to near the sideline (Diagram 138).

(Diagram 138)

(3) Goal kicker passes the ball to player 2, who further passes it to player 6 (Diagram 139).

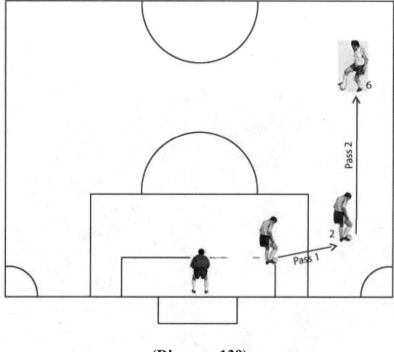

(Diagram 139)

Chapter 12:
Basic Principles of Soccer Game

Introduction

Soccer involves relatively complex strategies for effective play in competition. Each of the eleven field players has unique responsibilities and requirements. Thus, a coach must understand these unique responsibilities so that he/she can recruit the right athlete for the right position and design the proper training regimen for each athlete. Furthermore, how a coach sets up his/her team's formation and strategies should be base that team's specific circumstances and the opposing team's skill level. An effective coach will adjust the strategies for every game based on the opposing team's characteristics. Without a thorough knowledge of the various principles of soccer competition, coaches are unable to help athletes develop proper game perspectives and are also unable to design proper strategies for competition. This chapter covers many imperative principles of playing soccer games including: (1) soccer formation analysis, (2) position analysis, and (3) smart play at different zones of the soccer field. Once each athlete understands the requirements of his/her positions, his role on the team, and the position characteristics and particular responsibilities at different zones of the field, he/she can react to game situations much more effectively.

Soccer is a sport that requires balanced sport event between motor ability and cognitive intelligence; therefore, a successful soccer coach should not only teach athlete proper technical skills and proper physical training but also teach cognitive training such as the principles of competition. This chapter provides imperative information on competition principles that every coach and player must understand in order for the team to excel in competition.

Formation Analysis

▶ **The purpose of formation** is to clarify each player's responsibility during competition. A well-designed formation is the foundation for success in competition and should be modified based on the opposing team's situation.

► **Types of Formation**

(1) Formation of 4 - 4 - 2

Formation of 4 - 4 - 2 includes four defenders, four midfielders, and two offenders. Such a formation places a great emphasis on defense and controls the center region of the soccer field. Usually, when playing a strong team, a formation of 4-4-2 would be a good choice, not only because such a formation places a strong force on the center of the field, but also because it provides a strong defense line. When attacking, two midfielders can immediately become offensive players. The following is an illustration of the 4-4-2 formation (Diagram 140).

Formation 4-4-2

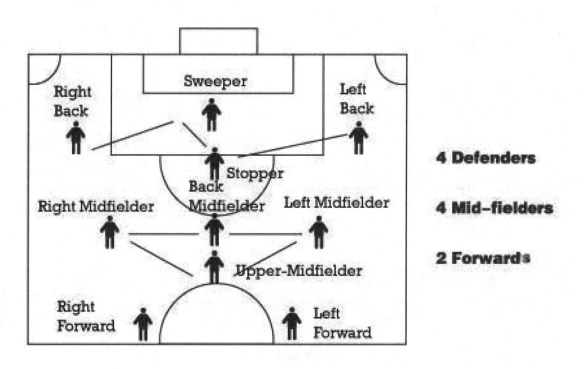

(Diagram 140)

(2) Formation 4 - 3 - 3

Formation of 4 - 3 - 3 includes four defenders, three midfielders, and three offenders. This type of formation is optimal when playing a relatively weak team, because it allows more offensive players to initiate attack. Meanwhile, three midfielders are available to control the central region of the field and organize the game effectively since the opposing team is not that strong. Four defenders would have enough security to defend the goal area. The following is a diagram of this formation (Diagram 141).

Formation 4-3-3

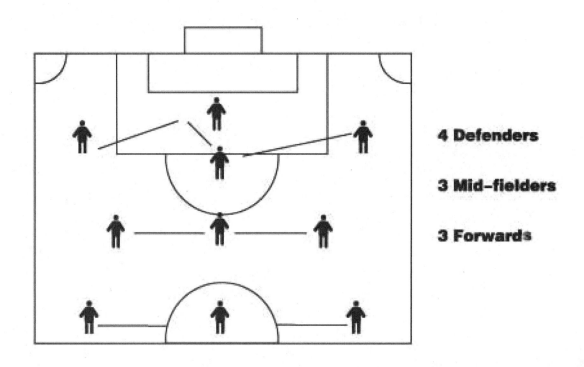

(Diagram 141)

(3) Formation of 5 - 4 - 1

Formation of 5 - 4 - 1 places significant emphasis on defense and the midfield
area. This formation attempts to provide the most secure strategy for preventing
the opponent from scoring during a competition. When attacking, some defenders
become midfielders and some midfielders become forwards. Such a formation has
become more and more popular in international competition (Diagram 142).

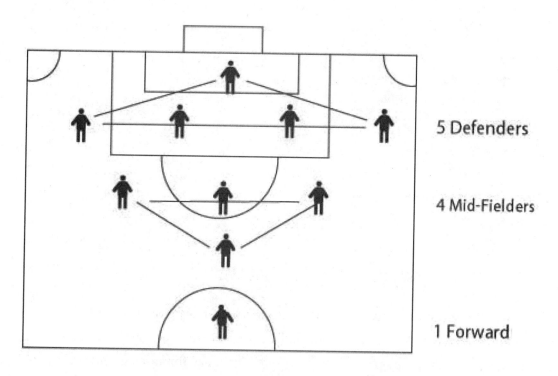

(Diagram 142)

(4) Formation of 4 - 5 – 1

Formation of 4 - 5 – 1 places great emphasis on the defense line and midfield area. This formation is often used in high-level competition (Diagram 143).

Formation 4 - 5 - 1

4 Defenders

5 Mid-fielders

1 Forwarder

(Diagram 143)

At the high school and college level in the U.S., many coaches like to play relatively aggressive games so they reluctently place more players on the defense line and midfield lines. Instead, they prefer to place more players as forwards in order to score the goals. These coaches usually like to use the formation of 4 - 2 - 4 or 4 - 3- 3. In fact, these formations expose a great weakness in the defense line and the teams that use these formations are likely to lose their games even though they might dominate the game most of the time due to the weakness of the defense line. This is because of the weak defense line. A conservative formation would first ensure the opposing team does not score, and next allow the team to score goals. Since soccer has a relatively low scoring rate, it is extremely difficult for a team who gives up a goal to turn around the momentum and immediately even the score. Hence, a strong defense line is an important strategy for the success in today's competitive soccer arena.

Position Role Analysis

▶ **Goalie**

The goalie's main responsibility is to prevent the opposing team from scoring goals. Goalies can use any part of their bodies including feet, hands, and arms during competition. However, the privilege of using the hands is limited to the penalty area.

▶ **Criteria for Selecting an Elite Goalie**

A goalie must possess a quick reaction time, jumping ability, flexibility, reasonable height, optimal weight (not too heavy), good decision-making ability, eye-hand coordination, and quickness of movement.

▶ **Left Full Back**

The main responsibilities of the left full back include: (1) defend the left side of the defense field to ensure the right forward of the opposing team is not able to penetrate through this side of the field. (2) assist the midfielders and forwarder to attack and sometimes act as a left forward in attacking, and (3) work closely with the left and center midfielders, sweeper, goalie, and stopper to protect the left-back zone of the field.

▶ **Right Full Back:**

The main responsibilities of the right full back include: (1) defend the right side of the defense field to ensure the left forward of the opposing team will not be able to penetrate through this side of the field; (2) assist the midfielders, and sometimes act as a right forward, and (3) work closely with right and center midfielders, sweeper, goalie, and stopper to protect the back-left zone of the field.

▶ **Stopper**

The abilities of the stopper include: (1) the physical strength to disrupt the opposing forwards' attack; (2) sufficient height to control air-balls in order to secure the back area of the field; and (3) good vision and perception to stay in good positions and make wise decisions when and where he/she needs to block, (4) work closely with midfielders, sweeper, and left and right full backs.

▶ Sweeper

The sweeper must have excellent basic soccer skills, good decision-making abilities, and quickness on the field, excellent tackling abilities, skills at clearing the ball, and the ability to organize well. The sweeper's skill level and intellectual abilities should be the best on the team because of the importance of his/her position. The sweeper's position is just before the goalpost, thus he/she serves as the last line of defense except for the goalie. The sweeper is responsible for securing the back area and protecting it from the opponents' attempts to score. Also, the sweeper can view the entire field and is able to organize the game well.

▶ Midfielders

The midfielders are considered organizers for the team during competition. They decide how, when and where to initiate an attack. These players must have great ball control skills, excellent decision-making abilities and a positive attitude toward teamwork. Also, the midfielders should have enormous physical ability because they have the dual responsibilities of defense and offense. When attacking, they play the role of offenders; while on defense, they become the main defensive players. How well midfielders play is a significant determinant of a team's success.

▶ Forwards

Forwards should have great individual skills such as dribbling, ball control, faking and beating opponents, shooting, creating opportunities for the teammates, perception of positioning, and so forth. One of the most effective strategies the offenders have is to dribble the ball to penetrate the opposing team's defense line for scoring. The forwards' running speed and ability to beat opponents should be the two most important talents they can possess. They should also work closely with the midfielders to break through defense the line to score goals.

Smart Play at Different Zones of the Soccer Field

The soccer field can be divided into three different zones: defense zone, midfield zone, and offense zone. Each of these zones demands unique characteristics of play. Every player must fully understand the principles of play relative to the respective zones in order to achieve maximum performance. If a player has great skills but lacks an understanding of the principles of play, his/her contribution to the team will be limited. An effective coach must not only structure skill training but also needs to teach athletes game principles based on the zone characteristics (Diagram 144).

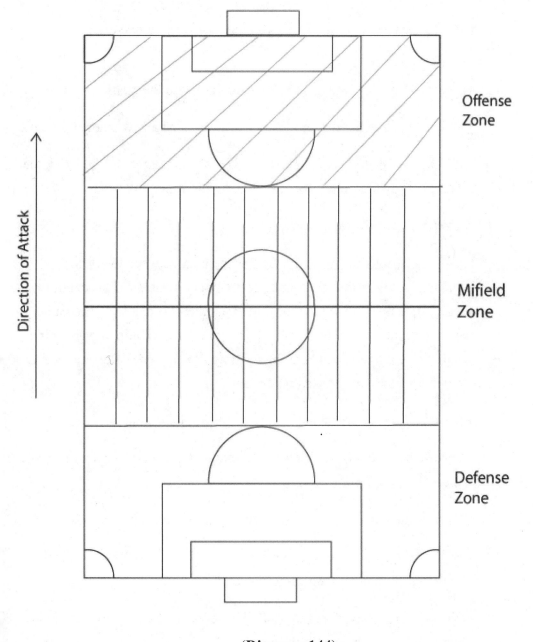

(Diagram 144)

▶ **Smart Play at Defense Zone**

The defense zone extends from the endline of the defense field to ten feet above the upper line of the penalty area. When the ball is in this area, the principles of defensive play are as follow:

- Whenever possible, avoid dribbling ball.

- Move the ball out of defense zone as soon as possible.

- Avoid passing the ball to the center of the goal area.

- A long pass is better than a short pass for clearing the ball out of the defense zone.

- Defensive players must closely collaborate with the goalie.

- Defensive players must eliminate or control air-balls whenever possible.

- If defensive players cannot possess the ball safely, they should kick the ball as far as possible to clear ball from this zone.

▶ **Smart Play at Midfield Zone**

The midfield zone of the soccer field is the area between the distance of the ten feet over the upper lines of both penalty areas. This central region of the field is the area for initiating attacks, organizing the game, distributing the ball to the right position for attack, creating opportunities for offensive players, and forming a strong defense line. Recommended play strategies in this area are as follows:

- Initiate attack or create opportunities for offensive players.

- Distribute the ball in a timely fashion to teammates rather than dribbling.

- Dribble the ball to create space and find the opportunity to pass.

- Play hard to dominate or control this area. The team that controls this region will dominate the game successfully.

- As soon as a player loses the ball, he/she must immediately engage in defensive play starting from this zone.

▶ Smart Play at Offense Zone

- Offense zone is the area that extends from the endline of the opposing team's field to ten feet above the upperline of the opposing team's penalty area. This zone, the best place for scoring, is the most competitive area for both teams because the offensive team wants to score goals there and the defensive team must play effectively to prevent goals from being scored. The following are the recommended strategies for playing in the offense zone:

- The offensive players can freely use dribbling skills to penetrate the defense line to score goals or force defensive players to commit fouls for free-kicks or penalty kicks.

- Watch out for off-side violations while the offensive players are preparing to receive the ball from teammates.

- Penetrate the defense line through the sideline, then pass the ball to the center for teammates to shoot on goal.

- Penetrate defense line through center field for shooting.

- Dribblers attract the defense players by creating opportunities for his/her teammates to score goal.

- Avoid passing in the offense zone to prevent errors.

- Complete shooting action even if the shooter's body has lost balance.

CHAPTER 13. INTERPRETATIONS OF SOCCER RULES

Introduction

     Understanding the rules of soccer is a must for every soccer player. The rules of soccer, from some perspectives, many seem relatively subjective and quite complex. Some soccer lovers who have involved in that sport for years may still be confused about the various soccer rules if they have not received proper training. For example, the rules of legal contact and offside are always difficult to understand, yet, confusion over these rules could cause a team to lose the competition. Many arguments occur both on and off the field between athletes and referees, between coaches to coaches, between audience to referees, and between parents and referees because of the misinterpretations of the rules of soccer. A thorough understanding of the rules of soccer will ensure not only avoids illegal play but also effectively uses those rules in competition to gain advantage within the legal perimeters. The following interpretations of major soccer rules provide a great opportunity for players to accurately understand the spirit and nature of the most crucial soccer rules.

Basic Knowledge of Playing Field

▶ **Diagram of a Standardized Soccer Field**

• **Units of the Measurement:** English System (Diagram 145).

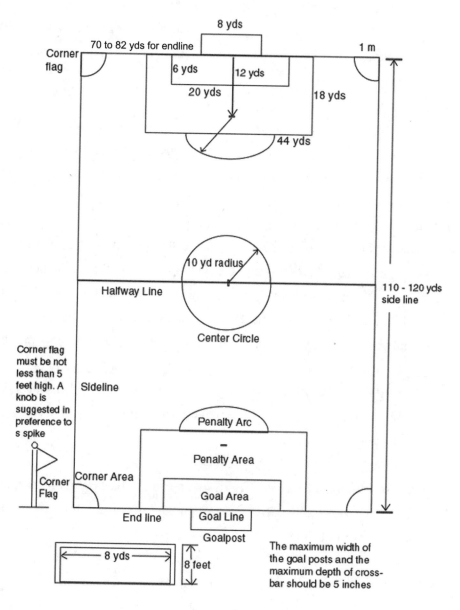

(Diagram 145)

▶ Functions of Each Area of a Soccer Field

(1) Goal Post

- If an entire ball was passed over the goal line into the goal post regardless of a ground ball or an air-ball, a goal was scored.
- Whether a goal is made, it depends on if an entire ball went into to the goal post instead of looking at a goalie's position. If a goalie stands inside of the goal post, but the ball is outside of the goal post, no goal is made, and vice versa.

(2) Goal Area

- It is the area where the ball should be placed in for a goal kick. When the ball is kicked over the right side of the end line of the field by an offender, the ball should be placed in the right side of the goal area for a goal kick and vice versa.

(3) Penalty Area

- The goalie has a privilege to use his/her hands within the penalty area.
- The player who takes a goal kick must kick the ball past the penalty box before the second player on either team can contact the ball. After the ball is kicked out from the penalty area, the game officially re-starts.
- If any defense player violates one of the direct free kick fouls in the penalty box, the offense team is awarded for a penalty kick.
- During the penalty kick, only the goalie and penalty kicker can stay in the penalty area and the rest of the players from both teams must stay outside of the penalty area.

(4) Side Lines

- A ball is kicked out, regardless if it is a ground ball or an air-ball, past the side line and the other team re-starts the game with a throw-in at the spot the ball went out.

(5) End Lines

- If a ball is kicked out, regardless if it is a ground ball or an air-ball, past the end line by a defense player, the offense team is awarded a corner kick. If a ball is kicked out, regardless a ground ball or an air-ball, past the end line by an offense player, the defense team is award a goal kick to re-start the game.

(6) Penalty Arc Area

- During the process of a penalty kick, all the players from both teams except the defense goalie and penalty kicker must stay outside of the penalty box.

(7) Center or Halfway Line

- Each player on both teams must stay in his/her own half of the field before the kickoff for starting a game.
- It is used for the offside rule that only happens on the opponent half side of the field.

(8) Center Circle

- Before the kickoff, all the players on the defense team must stay outside of the center circle. Once a ball is kicked off and makes one full rotation, the game officially starts.

(9) Corner Area

- The ball is placed in the corner area for a corner kick.

(10) Corner Flag

- The corner flags are located in each of the four corners to identify the boundary lines.

Interpretations of Soccer Rules

(1) Time of Soccer Game

- An entire soccer game lasts ninety-minutes - 45 minutes for each half of the game.
- A fifteen-minute break occurs between the first and second halves.
- If a soccer game tied, a thirty-minute overtime game, divided into two fifteen-minute halves, is played. A five-minute break occurs between the two halves.
- If a soccer game is temporarily stopped due to a fault or an out-of-bounds ball, the time of stopped play is counted as except in special situations such as injuries, arguments between referees and players, and so forth. In such situations, the head referee decides how much long the game should be extended because of the incident.

(2) Soccer Players

- According to the FIFA soccer rules, each soccer team may have a maximum of eleven players on the field during competition. A team can still compete with a minimum number of seven players if some are lost due to injury or red card(s).
- A total of eighteen players (eleven starters and seven non-starters) may be included on a team's roster for the World Cup competition.
- During an international soccer game, each team is allowed to substitute two

players. Once a player is substituted, he/she cannot be substituted again during that game.

- American colleges and high schools have different rules of substitutions.

(3) Soccer Rules for Field Players

- All field players are allowed to contact the ball with their entire body, except for arms and hands. If the soccer ball hits a player's arm or hand unintentionally, it should not be called a foul.

(4) Soccer Rules for Goalie

- Goalies can use their entire body to contact the ball, including arms and hands within the penalty area.

(5) Goal Kick

- When a ball is kicked beyond the endline by an offensive player, the defensive team must re-start the game with a goal kick.

(6) Corner Kick

- When a ball is kicked beyond the endline by a defensive player, the offensive team must re-start the game with a corner kick.

(7) Starting a Game from the Center

- An offensive player must kick the ball forward. When rolling ball completes a full rotation, the game has officially begun. Before a game starts, all the defensive players must stay behind their own center circle and behind the midline of the field.

(8) Direct Free Kick

- An offensive player can score a goal directly without having a second player contact the ball.
- If a defensive player commits one of the following fouls, the offensive team is awarded a direct free kick.

  1) A defensive player kicks or attempts to kick an offensive player.
  2) A defensive player traps or attempts to trap an offensive player.
  3) A defensive player steps on or attempts to step on an offensive player.
  4) A defensive player contacts or attempts to contact an offensive player for the purpose of knocking down an opponent instead of getting the ball.
  5) A defensive player contacts or attempts to contact an offensive player from behind.
  6) A defensive player contacts or attempts to contact an offensive player while jumping into the air.
  7) A defensive player hits or attempts to hit an offensive player.

8) A defensive player pushes or attempts to push an offensive player.

9) A defensive player grasps or attempts to grasp an offensive player.

10) A defensive player intentionally commits a hand ball.

(9) Indirect Free Kick

- The offensive player cannot score a goal directly; a second player must contact the ball before it goes into the goal.
- If a defensive player commits one of the following fouls, the offensive team is awarded an indirect free kick.
  1) Violation of the off-side rule.
  2) Dangerous play.
  3) Obstruction of play.

(10) Penalty Kick

- When a defensive player commits one of the fouls related to the direct free kick, the offensive team is awarded a penalty kick.
- During the penalty kick, no player can be positioned within the penalty area or the penalty arc area except for the goalie and the penalty kicker.

(11) Dangerous Play

- A player's action that could potentially cause his/her own injury or an opponent's injury is called a dangerous play.

(12) Obstruction of Play

- When a player's main objective is to use his/her body to block an opponent's attempt to get the ball, his/her action is called an obstruction.

(13) Red Card

- If a soccer player commits a serious violation of legal play or improper behavior on the field, he/she should receive a red card and be expelled from the competition.

(14) Yellow Card

- If a soccer player commits a relatively serious violation of illegal play or improper behavior on the field, he/she should receive a yellow card and can continue to play the game.

(15) Improper Behaviors

- The following behaviors are examples of improper behaviors: arguing with referees, yelling at teammates or opponents, intentional delay of game, cursing, showing disrespectful nonverbal behaviors, and so forth.

(16) Offside Rule

- When an offensive player meets all of the following situations, he/she has committed an offside foul:

   (a) The offside player's position must be in the defense team's half field.

   (b) Fewer than two defensive players are positioned the end line and the offside player.

   (c) The offside player is in a position ahead of the ball.

   (d) The offside should be called only when the player is passing the ball. There is no offside rule before the ball is passed or after the ball has been passed.

   (e) An offside foul should be called if the offside player obtains the advantage in the offside position. If an offside player has no advantage in that position, the referee should not call an offside foul.

1) **An Offside Situation:** During the moment of passing by player 6, there are less than two defenders in front of offensive player 8. An offside play should be called (Diagram 147).

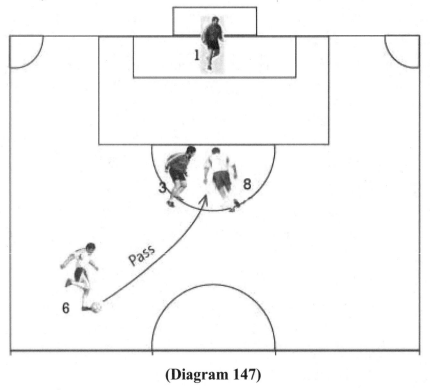

(Diagram 147)

2) A Non Offside Situation: During the <u>moment of passing</u> by offensive player 6, his teammate, player 10, is at a non offside position and he is running forward to head the ball at an offside position. This is not an offside play, because player 10 is at a non offside position during the <u>moment of passing</u> by player 6 (Diagram 148).

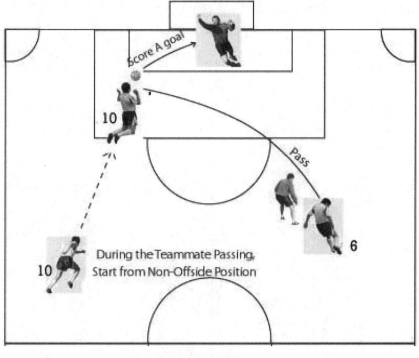

(Diagram 148)

3) An Offside Situation: During the <u>moment of passing</u> by offensive player 8, his teammate, player 10, is at an offside position and he is running backward to receive the ball at a non offside position. This is an offside play, because player 10 is at an offside position during the <u>moment of passing</u> by player 8 even though player 10 receives the ball at a non offside position (Diagram 149).

OffSide

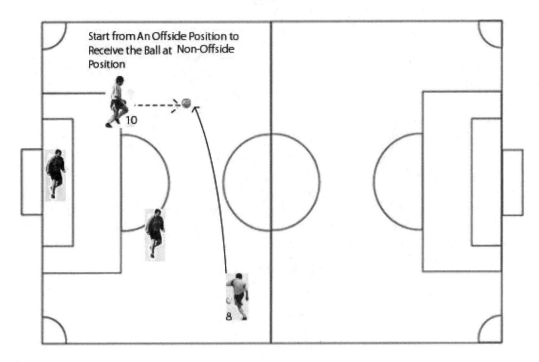

(Diagram 149)

References

Harter, S. (1978). Effectance motivation reconsidered: Toward a developmental model, Human Development, 21, 34-64.

Harter, S. (1981). A model of intrinsic mastery motivation in children: Individual differences and developmental change. In A. Collins (Ed.), Minnesota symposium on child psychology (Vol. 14, pp. 215-255). Hillsdale, NJ: Erlbaum.

Wang, J. (1999). Techniques for successful soccer shooting, Journal of Strategies. Vol. 13, No. 1, p. 17 – 20.

Wang, J. (2004). Application of scientific principles to advanced training of soccer-shooting, International Journal of Football and Science. Vol. 2, No. 1

About the Author

Dr. Jin Wang is a professor of Sport Science at Kennesaw State University, Atlanta, Georgia, USA. He was a former professional soccer athlete in China and was a successful head varsity soccer coach at the collegiate level in the U.S. Beyond his experiences as an elite athlete and coach, Dr. Wang is also a distinguished sport scientist who has published over forty sports journal articles and has made over eighty presentations at international and national conferences in the areas of soccer, sport skill training and sport psychology. Dr. Wang was an invited keynote speaker for the International Congress of Soccer & Science and was an invited speaker for the Olympic Solidarity Program sponsored by the International Olympic Committee. Currently, Dr. Wang is a Registered Sport Psychology Consultant for the United States Olympic Committee and the Chinese Olympic Committee and has worked with many world-class Olympic athletes from both countries. Dr. Wang is also the Chair of the Executive Committee of the Coaches' Council for the National Association of Sport and Physical Education (NASPE) and Research Consortium Fellow of American Alliance for Health, Physical Education, Recreation and Dance (AAHPERD) and serves as a reviewer for five international and national refereed journals. Dr. Wang received the 2005 Distinguished Scholar Award of the Southern District of the American Alliance for Health, Physical Education, Recreation and Dance in addition to many other awards.

Besides playing soccer, Dr. Wang also likes table-tennis, basketball, running and other physical activities. Dr. Wang is married and has two daughters and a son. Currently, he lives in Atlanta, Georgia in the United States. He can be reached by e-mail: wang566@gmail.com or phone: (770)-419-6161.

The author appears in the beautiful visual photos in this book.